CHARLES IVES
AND THE AMERICAN MIND

Charles Ives
and the
American Mind

ROSALIE SANDRA PERRY

THE KENT STATE UNIVERSITY PRESS

Publication of this book was assisted by the American Council of Learned Societies under a grant from the Andrew W. Mellon Foundation.

For my mother.

CONTENTS

FOREWORD

Today, one hundred years since his birth and twenty years after his death, Charles Ives is still the great enigma of American music. While the extraordinary originality and communicative power of his music are universally acknowledged, the man himself remains largely a mystery, and his relation to American culture a subject of continuing controversy. Was he, according to the early legend, a "rugged individualist", going his own way in defiance or scorn of established norms? Or was he, as a recent historian asserts, "a prisoner of his own culture", narrowly bound to institutions and values that stifled his career as a creative artist?

Such questions, and many others concerning Charles Ives as man and musician, will be much debated, both in the present year of his centenary and for decades to come. In the process a legend may disappear, but it is unlikely that interest will diminish or controversy be quelled. Ives was too vital a character to be historically quiescent.

Virtually unknown as a composer during most of his lifetime, Ives achieved recognition slowly, after he had ceased to compose and when it seemed that most if not all of his music might fall into total neglect. Having chosen a career in business rather than making music his profession, he lived until the late 1920's almost entirely apart from the professional world of music. He tried on various occasions to interest conductors and performers in his music, but the results were so discouraging—and in some instances humiliating—that he eventually abandoned such attempts.

After 1918, when he suffered a serious heart attack, Ives did very little composing. In 1927 he told his wife that he "couldn't seem to compose any more—nothing went well—nothing sounded right." Soon thereafter he ceased to be active in the insurance business that had made him wealthy, his health deteriorated further, and except for occasional travel he lived in comparative seclusion. He never heard a full orchestral performance of any of his major works.

The story of belated recognition is told in the time-lag between composition and performance. The Second Symphony, completed in 1897–1901, was first performed in 1951 (by Leonard Bernstein and the New York Philharmonic-Symphony). The Third Symphony, composed 1901–1904, received its première in 1945, with Lou Harrison conducting the New York Little Symphony. The Fourth Symphony, written between 1910 and 1916, had its first complete performance on April 26, 1965, under the direction of Leopold Stokowski. The Second Piano Sonata ("Concord"), composed from 1904 to 1915, had its first complete public performance by John Kirkpatrick in New York on January 20, 1939. The following day Lawrence Gilman, influential critic of the Herald-Tribune, hailed the work as "the greatest music composed by an American." This marked a major breakthrough in the recognition of Ives as *the* great American composer.

It is true that some fairly important performances had taken place earlier. In 1927 the first two movements of the Fourth Symphony were performed in New York under the direction of Eugene Goosens, sponsored by the Pro Musica Society. Ives now had active champions, notably the French-American pianist E. Robert Schmitz, founder and director of the Pro Musica Society; the composer Henry Cowell, who first met Ives in 1927; and the conductor Nicolas Slonimsky, all of whom did much to promote his music. In 1931–32, Slonimsky conducted several orchestral works by Ives in Paris, Berlin, Budapest, New York, Boston and Los Angeles. A number of these concerts were organized by the Pan-American Association of Composers (1928–34), which also sponsored a series of programs over Radio Station WEVD in New York that included various pieces by Ives and a movement of the First Piano Sonata.

In 1932, on the initiative of Aaron Copland, seven songs by Ives were included in the first Festival of Contemporary American Music held at Yaddo, an estate in Saratoga Springs, New York. The critical response was generally favorable and in some cases highly laudatory. "Charlie Rutlage" stole the show—which surely did not displease Ives.

By this time Ives was participating effectively—if vicariously—in American musical life, by being a generous patron of such "avant-garde" enterprises as the Pro Musica Society, the Pan American Association of Composers and Cowell's *New Music Quarterly*, founded in 1927 for the publication of "ultra modern" music.

Among the first to write appreciatively of Ives' music, in the 1920's and 1930's were his friend Henry Bellamann, the critics Olin Downes, Lawrence Gilman, and Paul Rosenfeld; Henry Cowell, and Bernard Herrmann, a composer and conductor. It was Herrmann who in 1932 called Ives "The Walt Whitman of American Music." Bellamann's article in *The Musical Quarterly* (January 1933), "Charles Ives: The Man and His Music", did much to establish the image of Ives as a man for whom "the fabric of existence weaves itself whole." According to Bellamann, Ives saw no contradiction or conflict whatever between his work in business and his dedication to music.

In the 1940's the chorus of appreciation was joined by Goddard Lieberson, Elliot Carter, Charles Seeger, W. H. Mellers (an English voice), Peter Yates, Lou Harrison, and others. In 1949 an article by Howard Taubman, "Posterity Catches Up With Charles Ives", appeared in the *New York Times Magazine*, with the subheading, "A distinguished composer who was in advance of the avant-garde looks back at a busy life." Ives was presented as "the most audacious pioneer in music that this country has produced." Thus the fame of Ives grew apace as it reached the mass media.

Official recognition came to Ives when, in 1947, he was awarded the Pulitzer Prize for his Third Symphony. Two years later he was elected a member of the National Institute of Arts and Letters.

In the early 1950's, when I was finishing my book, *America's Music* (published in 1955), I was puzzled as to where to place Ives, for he did not fit into the "proper" chronological sequence, having nothing in common with his academic contemporaries. So I placed him in a chapter by himself, anachronistically the last, to signify that he represented both a culmination and a new beginning in American music.

In the same year (1955), Henry and Sydney Robertson Cowell published the first full-length study, *Charles Ives and His Music,* which remained unique and authoritative for the next two decades. By

1958, Harold Schonberg could proclaim Ives to be "America's Greatest Composer" in the hospitable pages of *Esquire.*

The 1960's were the decade of apotheosis, culminating in the triumphant première of the Fourth Symphony and its subsequent presentation on more than one hundred stations of the National Educational Television network (December 1965–March 1966). Ives appeared as "An American Original" in David Hall's portrait in *HiFi/Stereo Review,* and Wilfred Mellers viewed him from England as an "American Hero"—comparable in music to Melville, Hawthorne, Thoreau, and Whitman in literature.

Meanwhile, the 1960's and 1970's saw an upsurge of scholarly interest in the music of Ives, with doctoral dissertations far outnumbering those on any other American composer. The most significant fact, however, is that some of these dissertations were done outside the domain of musical analysis and musicology. For example, a dissertation by Donald H. Frantz, "Search for Significant Form, 1905–1915: An Evaluation of the Symbols of Tradition and Revolt in American Literature, Painting, and Music" (University of Southern California, Department of Religion, 1960), took Ives as the representative figure in music.

In 1970, Frank R. Rossiter, a cultural historian, completed his dissertation on "Charles Ives and American Culture: The Process of Development, 1874-1921", in the Department of History at Princeton University. In 1971 Rosalie Sandra Perry completed her dissertation on "Charles Ives and American Culture", in the Department of History (American Civilization) at the University of Texas at Austin. Also in 1971, William Brooks completed his thesis on "Billings, Ives and Cage" at the University of Illinois in Urbana-Champaign. Though he worked within the School of Music, Brooks' approach—like Perry's—is that of cultural history from the viewpoint of a trained musician.

Sandra Perry is to be commended for undertaking in such a comprehensive framework the most challenging and difficult task that faces the historian of American music today: "To treat music as a functioning part of a wider whole" (Alan P. Merriam).

The cultural historians have brought us a greater awareness of the relation between American music and American culture. But it is well to remember that in this process of rediscovery and reinterpretation, Ives was the catalyst.

Gilbert Chase

ACKNOWLEDGEMENTS

I WOULD LIKE TO THANK DR. ROBERT M. Crunden for his insight and guidance in developing this topic. His far-ranging interests and practical help with sources and writing were very valuable to me, and my debt to him is profound.

Dr. Bryce Jordan and Dr. Delmer Rogers of the University of Texas Department of Music gave me special assistance and much helpful encouragement during my long period of writing. Both read several versions of the manuscript and made many valuable suggestions. I am grateful to Dr. Palmer Wright for his criticism and close reading of the manuscript; to the University of Texas for their research grant to Yale, and to John Kirkpatrick for his help while I was at Yale.

I would also like to thank Vivian Perlis, reference librarian at the Yale University School of Music, for her assistance in locating materials in the Ives' collection, and Eulan V. Brooks, librarian of The University of Texas for his many services. For other aid I am obliged to Dr. Frank Rossiter of The University of Michigan, and Dr. Johannes Riedel of The University of Minnesota.

I am very much indebted to Dr. Daniel E. Rider for his ideas in his dissertation on the Transcendentalist's musical thought and for leading me to primary sources I might otherwise have missed; to Dr. William Kay Kearnes' work for his insight and analysis of Horatio Parker, and to Dr. John C. Burnham and Dr. George Nathan Hale, whose dissertations provided certain ideas and other sources on the psychoanalytic movement in America. I also wish to acknowledge my debt to Dr. Robert Humphrey for several of his ideas on the stream-of-consciousness devices, and to Martha Doty, for initially calling my attention to revivalism in Ives' music.

In completing a book as wide-ranging as this one, I find my intellectual debts expanding to include persons too numerous to mention, but whose research (included in the bibliography) contributed both ideas and information on various topics covered here. To them, as to the others specifically mentioned, I express my appreciation for help so generously given.

For permission to quote parts of their published music, I would like to thank:

Mercury Music Corporation, Theodore Presser Co.

"Anti-Abolitionist Riots"

Merion Music, Inc., Theodore Presser Co.

"Thoreau"

"At the River"

"Soliloquy"

"Walt Whitman"

"Like a Sick Eagle"

"The Greatest Man"

"December"

"Tom Sails Away"

"A Farewell to Land"

"General William Booth Enters Heaven"

"Cradle Song"

"The Majority"

"Lincoln the Great Commoner"

Associated Music Publishers, Inc.

"Second Piano Sonata"

"Fourth Violin Sonata"

"Symphony No. 3"

"Symphony No. 4"

Sandra Perry
June, 1973

INTRODUCTION

In spite of a plethora of musical analyses, Charles Ives remains one of the most elusive forces of the early twentieth century. One can, with patience, dissect his technique, his life, and his musical impact. But the Ives that typified the junction between the nonconformist tendencies of the Romantic movement, its subsequent decay into genteel sentimentality, and what we call the Progressive Era, has received little attention. Yet Ives' artistic identity is far more comprehensible when viewed against his background than when removed from it and considered solely in the context of individual genius.

Ives interacted with the intellectual patterns of the culture of America and firmly believed that life should be an integrated whole, that aesthetic, moral, intellectual, and practical activities coalesce and fuse. The interplay of forces in Ives' music which so often results in a combination of insight and awkwardness represents, collectively, the use of various portions of both his past and the American past. The purpose of this study is to grasp more fully the interaction between this man, his music, and the American society of the past century. Ives was alert, intelligent, and well-read, the kind of man who was very much the product of intellectual trends and impulses in American civilization. His position was such that he could absorb a large portion of the life of his time, and his music profits from a study of this background.

Although many consider Ives as a musical pioneer—and his music did anticipate the developments of Stravinsky, Schoenberg, and Hindemith—the most important aspect of Ives' music lies in its expression of traditional American values of the past. Even the music's most avant-garde expression, pragmatism, was but "a new name for an old way of thinking". Ives' music was "about" something; almost all of it was so-called program music about the American past, a past that he often viewed nostalgically through his childhood. In a sense, Ives' music is "about" memory and submerged, half-remembered episodes in his consciousness. *Holidays,* for example, describes Ives' recollections of festivities in a Connecticut country town.

In this attempt to recast the operation of Ives' mind within his tradition, five uses of the past appear to dominate his musical and intellectual thought. First, Ives' personal past led him naturally to innovation within common, awkward forms. From his father, George, a musical jack-of-all-trades, he learned to experiment with new sounds and combinations of sounds. Along with his enthusiasm for musical experiment, Charles learned to love the informal, amateur, and popular musical culture of the small American town. Songs of the camp meeting, rural dance tunes, band marches, and the cacophony of country Fourth of July celebrations filled his mind with imagery he would later recapture and transform in compositions filled with quotations.

Later at Yale, which he entered in the fall of 1894, Charles entered into the classical, genteel, music world. This world was somewhat atypically represented by Horatio Parker, Ives' teacher, who was a well-known American composer and member of the "Boston Classicists", a group of composers whose works generally followed the canons of European training. Parker's chief influence on Ives was primarily due to his lectures, which often reiterated the dogmas of Transcendentalism. He emphasized "substance", the foundation for music, as opposed to external mannerisms, and he disparaged sentimentality. The empirical process, Parker claimed, was the best guide for a composer, and in his own works he often experimented with opposing rhythms and tonalities. Parker also borrowed ideas and melodies from other composers, and many of his works contain quotations from popular songs as thematic material. All these germinal ideas grew to maturity in Ives' music and philosophy.

A second, rather obvious meaning of Ives' past lies in his use and interpretation of the Transcendental tradition. Many of Ives' ideas paralleled Emerson's, and Ives may even have patterned his own life-style after the great philosopher. Ives also borrowed many of Thoreau's ideas about what constitutes music.

Ives' preoccupation with Transcendentalism was not so much an indication of his aspiration to divinity as it was an attempt to delve into the subconscious. The subconscious, a transitionless flow, opened the door to Ives' stream-of-consciousness technique, which was a third meaning of the past that paralleled the doctrine of the unconscious advanced by such medical men as Morton Prince and William James.

With the blending of conscious and unconscious, of art and life, certain realistic techniques—more common to literature than music—arose. This realism was the fourth meaning of the past. Realism, a pluralistic term encompassing not only common subject matter, exactness of representation, and a moral orientation, but also the subjective side of man, was a kind of refusal to accept a dualist order of the conscious and the subconscious. Enlarging the scope of what is considered "real" to include memories, dreams, and nonobjective phenomena led Ives back through a past of utopian visions that Edward Bellamy had earlier explored in his famous novel, *Looking Backward.* Ives was not alone in pursuing a Messianic concept of social transformation. A number of his contemporaries, caught up in the chaotic changing society of 1880–1900, wanted to escape from the consciousness of the present, and progress to an evolutionary utopia. Transcending reality was a progressive and utopian goal that affected Ives' moral, intellectual, political, and social values and attitudes as well as his music.

Reality as an "ongoing process" was a characteristic of evolutionary thought, which, in effect freed the individual from an authoritative past independent of its present uses. This fifth use of the past was essentially based on the idea that change was the only constant, and environment something that could be manipulated. Before World War I blasted open the stability of progressive thought, Ives and his peers followed the trail blazed by Charles Sanders Peirce. Peirce's pragmatism, an application of evolutionary biology to human ideas, emphasized the study of ideas as instruments of the organism, and was an old way of thinking that fitted easily into the middle-class consciousness. Judgment by the result was one side of the coin of pragmatism; the other side was what Henri Bergson would call "intellect removed from fundamental reality and is best conversant with the solids which it cuts out from the continuous stream of experience and impulse." [1] As such, pragmatism was a refracting medium for many currents in American life, for it repudiated limiting definitions and consistency. In a sense, it was the old Transcendental denial of material reality and stress on the mind all over again. The sciences of physics and psychology reinforced the pragmatic idea that life was an unceasing, continuous, undivided process, a kind of universal movement of which we are expressions rather than parts. This idea of mind as a continuum helped bridge the gap between Eastern and Western philosophy, for Oriental philosophy developed the first interpretation of limitless consciousness. Indeed, with pragmatism, the circle was complete, for Transcendentalism originally triggered the merging of East and West with its metaphysics which propounded that All was One (the Over-Soul). It was one easy step from substance to process, and relations, in becoming more real and important than the things they relate, linked Oriental mysticism and American thought.

Ives' music reflects all these intellectual trends—Transcendentalism, the stream-of-consciousness, realism, and pragmatism—which are bound together by their preoccupation with time and thought as a process. The way in which his music relates to these nonmusical aspects may give access to further interpretive associations; yet this analysis may furnish significant clues for further insight into the composer's hitherto unknown mental processes and into the dynamisms of his successes and failures. This work is not a biography, a conventional history, or a work about the performance of music or music theory, but it does touch on these matters in the course of evaluating certain factors in intellectual history that have gone into the making of Charles Ives' music. In essence, this work is a test case for exploring the social psychology of music.

Ives' was a complicated, difficult mind. His detractors often find his published writing incomprehensible, and his music painful. He lived a respectable, genteel life, but his music was seldom considered good enough to be performed until recent years, when he finally came into his own. In fact, there already exists something that may be called an Ives cult, and he is no longer in danger of being neglected. On the contrary, too much is made of some of his works, music that should remain peacefully "in the leaf" as he himself might have said. I levy this charge against some of Ives' works because of my contention that many of his experiments were visual, free-association forms. Some were profound, parallel transformations of intellectual concepts into music. Some were not so successful, for as many would agree, the mind is capable of generating kitsch as well as art.

C. E. I.: THE PERSONAL PAST

He WAS TOUGH, NOBODY'S FOOL AND nobody's yes-man. From the beginning his music was wonderfully bound up with the very backbone of New England character, a character which is built upon contradictions. The wonder of it is that he, with his elaborately informed classical background and strong sense of the past, was ever dubbed a "primitive". Primitive he was not. He was not naive. He was not untrained. His education and background were the best heritage of German-American education available in North America.

The now-passé label of "primitive" may have been attached to him because of his sensuality. Yet this sensuality was deeply rooted in the rough-hewn, instinctive independence of the New Englander whose classic phrase was "every pot should stand on its own bottom." Despite his origins, his motley collections of works were generally regarded as eccentricities, and his parochialism even confounded his own townspeople who, along with everyone else, believed that "the only good music was European music." Characteristically, Ives withdrew. He was morally, economically, and sartorially devoted to old customs and ways of the past—but of his own past, not a Europeanized past. God may be everywhere, so Ives concurred with Emerson's Transcendentalism, but he was especially located in New England.

At every juncture, Ives stood in line with the past's extravagant diversity of New England eccentrics, from Thoreau at Walden to the irascible John Jacob Astor, who could casually remark that "a man with a million dollars is as well off as if he were rich."

Although no one in the New England village of Danbury, where Charles Ives was born, could compete with Astor in material wealth, some of his second-hand European standards filtered down to them. "Good music," for example, could be recognized by its dullness, stiffness, and meaninglessness. "Nice girls" had to play the piano; indeed, the sign of middle-class status was for one's marriageable daughter to be able to sing a little and play on the family upright which stood cloaked in a fringed, silk shawl in a prominent corner of the living room. "Good" music was precisely the product of the sentimentalizing taste of the nineteenth century, a taste fostered by the stereotyped Woman-as-Weakness-and-Harbinger-of-Gentility. Ives, like other males, felt the implications of this femininity and was partly embarrassed by his musical interests. The sarcasm that came easily to him aimed at the "feminine" in music and could not hide a basic insecurity in his make-up. When other boys on Monday mornings during vacation were out riding horses or playing ball, he felt peculiar when he stayed in to play the piano.[1] He was partially ashamed of being a musician and he knew it. This ambivalent feeling drove him to search for a music that could once again be recognized as masculine. Ives, his music and his career could only have happened in an America torn between the decaying sentimentality of a borrowed Victorianism and the surging progressivism that soon overwhelmed it.

Yet in reality his music was in many ways a throwback to a distant New England, admittedly, a New England of memory. Not that he would agree too readily to this, for like most Yankees he held the common belief that he had nothing in common with any of the others. But, in fact, he did. His father's family came from a sturdy captain of Dorchester, England—William Ives; who landed in Boston in 1635 and was one of the original party to settle Quinnipiac in Connecticut (now part of New Haven). The family remained in Connecticut for nine generations and numbered among its members such solid citizens as parsons, bankers, lawyers, and farmers. Charles' great-grandfather, Isaac Ives, a graduate of Yale, married Sarah Amelia White, daughter of a prominent Danbury family. Their son George White Ives was born in New York City. George White Ives' son, also named George, was a unique personality and a remarkable bandmaster who left a few compositions and many inventions, but none very practical.

The neighbors regarded George Ives as a crank, but he was no self-taught amateur. In 1860 he was studying with Carl Foeppl, a German musician who had a small farm in Morrisania, in the Bronx, and apparently receiving a thorough grounding in music. His notebooks show Bach chorales, parts of baroque masses, opera scenes from Gluck and Mozart as well as marches and band tunes. He had sound conventional training in music theory from a number of other teachers and could play almost any musical instrument. Moreover, he had absolute pitch, and this gift led him into experiments with quarter tones and different sound combinations. Much to his neighbors' dismay, he built a contraption to produce quarter tones out of twenty-four violin strings and a clothes-press. Like many of his inventions, it didn't work too well. In 1874 he married Mary Parmelee, whose father, appropriately enough, was a farmer-turned-inventor with a secret hope that one of his Sunday-inventions would solve the old dilemma of perpetual motion. There is no record of how the family regarded the marriage.

Charles Edward Ives was born on October 20, 1874 in Danbury, and was soon followed by a brother, Joseph Moss II, born in February 1876. Their mother proved to be a staunch New England housewife, concerned with appearances and the health of her family. Although she did not particularly share her husband's interest in music, she did not oppose it. Yet with lively George as his father, young Charles' life was far from bleak. He hung around his father's band rehearsals from the time he could walk, for he admired his father immensely. It seemed to him that a familiar tune meant more when his father played it. True, the things he played were the things that most bands played, but he put something in them that most band leaders did not.[2]

Young Charles had an extraordinary environment. One of his boyhood heroes was the country fiddler John Starr, and he heard fiddlers playing tunes for dances as well as performances of strenuous revival hymns, romantic four-part hymns, slow, methodically decorated psalms, sentimental parlor music, ballads, popular songs by Stephen Foster, and the chamber music of Handel, Bach, and Beethoven. Young Ives' own training in music started at the hands of an old German bandsman named Slier, who had played the drum in George Ives' Danbury Civil Band. Slier gave Charles an empty tub and a couple of drumsticks and taught him the double roll and all the other things a good drummer was expected to know. George Ives taught his son piano, violin, cornet, sight-reading, harmony, and counterpoint. Most important of all, Charles heard his father's explorations of acoustics, natural sounds, and new instrumental sounds, and gained the early practical experience with instruments in each category that gave him a knowledge of their possibilities that greatly exceeded the academic knowledge possessed by most composers at that time. These early years revealed an exceptional musical talent in the boy.

When he was twenty, his father died suddenly. It was a severe emotional blow for the boy, but he continued on at Yale, living in the home of J. C. Griggs, a friend of his father's. He spent his next four years at Yale, at this time an obdurately conservative, oligarchical, and old fashioned institution.[3] The government of Yale was dominated by Protestants and the faculty refused to experiment, for the college had always resented new ideas. Many of the faculty and government of Yale had fought the elective system and pushed the sciences and social sciences over into the Scientific School. The majority at Yale seemed to prefer discipline to free thinking, organization to originality, athlete to scholar. Yet the power of Yale was unmistakable and its order superlative.[4]

Ives' formal education proved strenuous. Every morning at ten minutes past eight every student had to be at chapel; at eight-thirty everyone recited. The College prescribed all the work of freshman and sophomore years, and Yale men sat together under the same teachers doing the same tasks. This compulsory system led George Santayana, a young Harvard instructor in 1892, to write that "The past of America makes itself felt there in many subtle ways: there is a kind of colonial self-reliance, and simplicity of aim, a touch of non-conformist separation from the great ideas and movements of the world." [5] But not only the past was "enshrined at Yale," the present was portrayed also:

> Nothing could be more American. . . . Here is sound, healthy principle, but no overscrupulousness, love of life, trust in success, a ready jocoseness, a democratic amiability, and a radiant conviction that there is nothing better than one's self. It is a boyish type of character, earnest and quick in things practical, hasty and frivolous in things intellectual. . . . No wonder that all America loves Yale, where American traditions are vigorous, American instincts are unchecked, and young men are trained and made eager for the keen struggles of American life.[6]

Observers other than Santayana made similar judgments: Yale was
a thoroughly conservative institution, traditional in its habits, religious in its spirit, earnest and moral in its atmosphere, conforming
in its opinions, old-fashioned in its education. And full of traditions.
According to Edwin E. Slosson, the past was not really the past
at Yale. It was part of the present.

> . . . Ask a Yale man the reason for anything and he will give you
> the origin; and he thinks he has answered your question. . . .
> "Why do all the dormitory windows have those big water bottles
>   in them?"
> "Because the city water was bad a few years ago."
> "Isn't it all right now?"
> "Oh, yes."
> "Why do the college students have to attend chapel every morning?"
> "They always have." [7]

Young Ives unavoidably found himself immersed into this
community. He was an active and sociable person, a member of
HeBoule, Delta Kappa Epsilon, and Wolf's Head. Although he
was a highly individualistic young man, the instinct for organization during the 1890s at Yale was strong. The undergraduates
constituted an almost "primitive brotherhood." "Together" was
the great word, and Yale stood for team play. The undergraduates
imitated the organizations and competitions of the outside world,
and within their groups each strove to establish certain values,
for the college preached and practiced the ideal of public service.
Yale, without a doubt, conformed. The Yale man's education did
not encourage him to be an individual, for his classmates thought
that cooperation was far more important than critical thought.
Campus sentiment discouraged all eccentricity of dress or conduct,
and tradition made it difficult for a man to rely on himself, or
go against the popular opinion. A man did not go to Yale just
for what he could get out of it, for individualism was discouraged
and originality of ideas was automatically suspect. This emphasis
on conformity and cooperation set Yale apart from other institutions. At Cambridge, for example, the Harvard man was apt to
be such a law unto himself that team play and concerted effort
were impossible. Other institutions welcomed the new and had
little use for old ways and ideas. But to succeed at Yale, men
had to avoid solitariness in thought and action. [8]

The same kind of puritanical, conservative, and moralistic approach that Yale had in regard to education was applied to the fine arts. The beginning of music at Yale was a musical club, formed in 1812, which later called itself The Beethoven Society. It furnished music at religious services, and in the chapel until 1855. The Beethoven Society used sacred texts for mixed chorus— the same sort of music that Lowell Mason had used. Such music was rhythmically bland, genteely correct in the European Classical style, and harmonically innocuous. This club supplied the chief opportunity for the study and practice of music at Yale until 1854, when Joseph Battell established a fund for the support of a teacher of the Science of Music. Gustave J. Stoeckel, appointed first as Instructor in Vocal Music, later became Chapel Master and Organist.[9] After he assumed these offices and consequently became director of the choir and glee club, he abandoned the kind of music that the Beethoven Society had been using, and music for male voices became the standard fare for the choir and glee club. From the beginning, the Department of Music at Yale had the status of a professional school under the administration of the larger university. The first courses to appear in the Yale Catalogue (1891–94) were developed and taught by Stoeckel:

I. *Harmony.* 2 hrs. both terms: acoustics, intervals, chords with inversions and combinations. Modulation. Nonharmonic tones. Suspensions. Accompaniment of a melody.

II. *Counterpoint, Canon, Fugue.* 2 hrs. both terms: counterpoint: single, double, triple, quadruple. Imitation, canon, fugue.

III. *Forms:* motive, phrase, period, part-song, rondo, sonata, orchestral forms.[10]

Also included in the curriculum were *Lectures on the History of Music and Aesthetics* which included analyses of the oratorio, opera, chamber-music, and the symphony.

After Dr. Stoeckel retired, Horatio William Parker (1863–1919) a composer of the so-called "Boston Classicist" school who had studied under George Chadwick and Josef Rheinberger, was appointed Battell Professor of the Theory of Music. Other music faculty members were Samuel Simons Sanford, Professor of Applied Music and Harry Benjamin Jepson, College Organist. At this time

(1894) the college included Practical Music in its curriculum as an elective.

When Horatio Parker took over, the course offerings were expanded from three to six. One of the courses that appeared in the *Catalogue of 1894* (the year Ives entered Yale) was "Free Composition" taught by Parker. There were a number of prerequisites, and the freedom to compose in a manner of one's own choosing came only after a careful disciplining in harmony, contrapuntal techniques, orchestration, and creativity in the smaller forms. Parker taught the *History of Music* course, although he was not at all sure that talk about music was profitable. "It is not always particularly profitable to talk about music, at least not for musicians. . . . It cannot be expressed in words at all," he wrote.[11] In summary, the *History of Music* course at Yale was taught in one of the oldest and most honored traditions of Western education. Its professor acquainted himself with the facts from the best sources available. He taught these facts, not as ends in themselves, but rather he reinterpreted them in terms of their significance in his own life.[12]

In 1894 the New Haven Symphony Orchestra also began its career, giving a series of orchestral concerts every year. Parker thought that the orchestra's primary function was to play student compositions, which gave an incentive to the student to compose and allowed him to hear what he had written. "It is as a laboratory for such," Parker wrote, "that I believe the orchestra fulfills its highest function." [13]

Parker's philosophy of music education emphasized a rigid, theory-dominated program of instruction. This was not typical of all music schools of the time. Many held the same position as Waldo S. Pratt, who urged a better general education for music students and a closer affiliation with other areas of learning in order to end what he called "the isolation of music." [14] Parker's uncompromising, rather antihumanistic position concentrated on the disciplinary aspects of music. The students felt towards Parker the same commingled feelings of admiration and fear typical of those studying in the German academic tradition in which he was trained.[15,16]

As a man, Parker was exactly opposite from what the public was used to. The public expected eccentricity, irresponsibility, a disheveled appearance, and discreetly immoral conduct from artist-performers. The adulation of virtuosos in the nineteenth century was an emphasis on the performer of music rather than the composer, and Parker, the composer, contradicted this stereotype, as did the other Boston Classicists. He was fastidious, immaculate, and a man of the world who commanded a social standing often denied musicians of his time. He had for his friends artists, writers, and men from the several professions—seldom musicians—and he could hold his own in prolonged discussions on topics far removed from music.[17]

Musically, one of the distinguishing characteristics of his art was his susceptibility to other composers' mannerisms. Mendelssohn, Franck, Liszt, Gounod, Brahms, Wagner, and Dvorak were often his models as well as certain Baroque and Renaissance composers.[18] "I firmly believe in permanent musical values," wrote Parker. "I think that those parts of Handel's *Messiah* which now please us most are exactly the ones which made the greatest impression on the very first audience which heard the work sung." Parker remarked that he did not know whether they were the parts that Handel himself wrote with greatest pleasure or at highest tension, "for a composer is at times a partly unconscious instrument who records beauties thrust upon him, flowing through him from heaven to earth. He does not always know what he writes, however perfect it may be. Seventeen-year-old Schubert writing the Earl King [19] cannot have known what he was making, although of course he loved it. But the high aim and simple integrity of great composers are no accidents. Such men have made themselves perfect instruments by their life and work and thought." [20]

Many ideas that Ives later states in his own work and as pieces of his own philosophy had their genesis in remarks of Horatio Parker. For example, Ives' preoccupation with "manner or substance" may have been initiated by Parker's emphasis on "form and substance" as the "more solid foundation for music".[21] Parker wrote that he thought that the art of absolute music was exhausted. The music of the Germans, he pointed out, was "colored by externals," while that of the French was superficial, and that of the Italians (opera) was a form of manifest limitation. He thought that all of them—Germans, French, and Italians—were trying to create an entirely new vocabulary. "So much that *they frequently lose sight of form and substance.*" Parker did not object to addition to music's means of expression, but he thought that the new vocabulary should always remain a means, and never become an end of expression.[22]

Parker also reacted strongly against sentimental, weak, and shallow music. "I want to advance the proposition that we can get used to anything. If we give people weak music they will accept it and love it," Parker wrote; "Likewise will they accept strong music, and love it infinitely better in the end, for they can also respect it." [23] Ives would later share the same feeling, and in his campaign for "strong, masculine music" he asserted his maleness and associated this belief with the ideal of democracy.

Many now consider Parker a pedant as a composer. Strangely enough, however, William Apthorp and other critics of his time frequently criticized Parker for not adhering closely enough to the established rules of composition. Likewise, an analysis of his addresses and public statements shows that the description of him as rigid and unchanging in his musical opinions is not quite accurate; he underwent a transformation from conservative, narrow views regarding the function of music in society to liberal opinions such as the justification of popular music and the advocacy of federal government support for the arts. Although music historians frequently describe Parker as a conservative, backward-looking composer, many of his major compositions were innovations in the sphere of American music. For example, the restless harmonies of his opera *Mona* disturbed the critics. Max Smith found in the harmony "a willful search for ugly dissonance which apparently has no psychological or dramatic point." [24] The New York *Sun* described its opposing rhythms and tonalities, and observed that the text seemed to float on a fluid stream of recitative: "The ceaseless change of tonality and the endless intrusion of opposing rhythms impart to the musical speech a singularly intangible character." [25]

Parker, like his student Charles Ives, frequently borrowed ideas both from himself and other composers. Kearnes dissects *A Wanderer's Psalm*, opus 50, an oratorio commissioned for The Three Choirs' Festival held at Hereford in 1900, and finds extensive fughetta sections similar to those of *Hora Novissima*; the melody of the soprano solo borrowed from the famous English horn solo of Cesar Franck's *Symphony in D Minor*; and the principal theme of the storm section borrowed from the opening motive of *Der fliegende Holländer.* Parker, like Ives, took pleasure in blending the sacred and the secular. His most famous work, *Hora Novissima,* written in 1893, resembles the works of other composers from the Renaissance masters to the European Romantics and contains passages in the Italian tradition of Pergolesi, Rossini, and Verdi. (The critics of the day criticized it for being too operatic.) There are nearly direct quotations such as the "Dresden Amen" in the coda of the first chorus *Hora Novissima,* p. 17, measures 1–7), or the sudden appearance of a fragment of the *Wedding March* from Mendelssohn's music to *A Midsummer Night's Dream* at the climax of the closing chorus to Part I. In a later work, *Collegiate Overture* (1911?), opus 72, Parker used several college songs popular at Yale as the thematic material. "Undertaker Song" is the principal theme, but "Boola" also appears in the introduction. Other songs that appear include "Eli Yale," "Amici," "Integer Vitae," "Gaudeamus Igitur," and "Here's to Good Old Yale."

Ives was merely following a tradition in his writing of compositions celebrating specific events and national holidays. Ceremonial works (so-called because they include a textual or musical feature peculiar to the occasion being celebrated) were popular among Americans long before Ives wrote such works as *Holidays, Washington's Birthday,* and so on. Two years after Ives was born (1874) a chorus of one thousand voices and a two hundred-piece orchestra performed Dudley Buck's *Centennial Meditation of Columbia,* written for the Philadelphia Exhibition of 1876. Horatio Parker, too, wrote a number of pieces in commemoration of specific events: *Ode for Commencement Day at Yale University 1895, Greek Festival Hymn* (1901), *Allegory of War and Peace* (1916) and *A. D. 1919.*

Parker's own unresolved contradictions led him to disparage sentimentality in music, but he was never able to divest himself of its mannerisms. Parker, unlike Ives, was a self-made intellectual. His grade school record was not distinguished, and there is no record of his having completed high school. Yet his burning desire for knowledge led him to the study that later won the respect of his colleagues at Yale, for he was determined to overcome the real and imagined deficiencies of his informal schooling. "Although he succeeded in doing so," wrote Kearnes, his best biographer, "one senses to some extent in his addresses and essays a lack of completely logical development, an unwillingness to explore ideas in great

depth, and a tendency toward premature generalization. . . ." [26]
Like many self-made intellectuals, Parker was impatient with the
culturally broadening courses of University curricula. As a result,
he was most emphatic among educators of the time in stressing
technical training not only for the composer and the professional,
but also for the layman as well.

The major difference between his earlier and later statements
is a matter of inclusiveness. Formerly (before 1920), Parker had
concerned himself only with a rather narrow segment of serious
music. In his later years he attempted to define a purpose for all
kinds of music and somehow or other to find a philosophical
position to include the complete musical scene. The pragmatism
that later emerged from Ives' work was inherent in Parker's earlier
philosophical position, for Parker insisted that the "empirical process" was a composer's only effective guide.[27] But it was 1900,
two years after Ives left Yale, before Parker made a basic change
in the curriculum of his theory course by de-emphasizing fig-
ured-bass writing and stressing the harmonization of melodies. He
now encouraged the student to discover "original principles" rather
than engage in rote learning of rules as suggested earlier. George
W. Chadwick's book, *Harmony*,[28] replaced Jadassohn's European-
oriented textbook.

"I had and have ["great" crossed out] respect and admiration
for Parker and most of his music," wrote Charles Ives. "It was
seldom trivial. His choral works have dignity and depth that many
contemporaries, especially in religious and choral compositions, do
not have." [29] Parker influenced Ives in many ways. First, his lectures
often reiterated the dogmas of Emerson and the Transcendentalists.[30] Ives wholeheartedly accepted these beliefs. The second
recurring theme in Parker's addresses, lectures, and private letters
was his belief in the necessity of progress.[31] Parker's generation
could be backward-looking, even as it tried to eliminate inequities
and injustices. This same kind of progressivism and "backward
looks" appeared in the writings and beliefs of his student, Charles
Ives. Ives also expanded Parker's beliefs in "strong music," "manner
and substance," and "the empirical process" or pragmatism.

Parker's musical influence showed up in two ways. First, Ives
reacted strongly against Parker's musical authoritarianism. Second,
Ives applied in his music many of Parker's philosophical ideas.

Parker's music with its occasional dissonances and Parker's use of borrowed tunes and musical styles possibly suggested to Ives the use that could be made of other composers' material.

Ives wrote his *First Symphony* as part of the requirements for Horatio Parker's composition course in 1898. The Symphony, a strangely uneven work, contained four movements in the accepted European symphony style. Yet it foreshadowed Ives' later works with its combination of keys in the first movement. Parker even made Ives rewrite this movement when he saw that the subject, supposed to be in D minor, passed through eight different keys. "The new end part seemed no good to me," wrote Ives when Parker also told him to rewrite the conclusion of the symphony following the classic symphonic form. "And I told Parker that I would much prefer to use the first draft. He smiled and let me do it, saying: "But you must promise to end on D minor!" [32] Yet while Ives labored to be conventional and echoed the European symphonists, developing his material in the style of Dvorak, Wagner, Brahms, and Strauss, the tapestry of melodies in the coda previews his incredible innovations.

After graduation from Yale in 1898, Ives went to New York where he started work for $5 a week as a clerk in the actuarial department of The Mutual Life Insurance Company. His decision to go into business was partly based on the Transcendental belief that the ordinary business of life was, itself, suffused with the highest ideals of spiritual life, that life was all of "one fabric". Practically, however, Ives knew that his experimental music would not earn him a living, and he was not interested enough in the dull and pompous European-style of music to devote himself to writing or teaching it. He preferred to go into business, and write music as he heard it, not influenced by monetary considerations. [33]

At this time he moved into an apartment on the fourth floor of 317 West 58th Street, between 8th and 9th Avenues, with a group of young men: William Darrach, James Judd, Harry Keator, James Lewis, Michael Gavin, George Schreiber, and Edward Sawyer. They called their place "Poverty Flat" (actually two apartments), and combined to pay the expenses. Ives also took a job as organist and choirmaster for the First Presbyterian Church in Bloomfield, New Jersey, and then for the Central Presbyterian Church on West 57th Street in New York, where he played for services from 1889-1902.

During these years Ives worked hard on his own compositions in his free time, often composing until two or three in the morning. After 1902 his manuscripts became like a huge diary and his music more experimental.[34] He seldom went to concerts because he found other composers' music disturbing to his own ideas, and too, his time was limited because his days were spent in business. On weekends he and his brother Moss used to camp out on a mountain top not far from Danbury; his other "nights-out" were spent playing ragtime in a beer garden with his friends or walking until daybreak in Central Park. During these years (1898–1918), he was highly prolific, writing music nearly every evening. Some of the pieces he produced include his *Second Symphony,* his *Third Symphony, The Celestial Country,* a cantata for mixed chorus, quartet, soli, strings, brass and organ, *The Concord Sonata, Holidays, Decoration Day, The Fourth of July, The Fourth Symphony, Three Places in New England,* and *The Robert Browning Overture.* Ives occasionally tried to have his works performed, but each of these attempts met with derision and adverse criticism. Finally, Ives retired to work by himself, completely isolated in his musical life.

Ives' opinion of music critics was, not surprisingly, very low. In a short paper called "Ode to a Music Critic" he referred to George (apparently a music critic) whose grandfather called him to his knee and said, "George, if you only knew jest a leetle bit more, you'd be half-witted." But Ives' opinion of his own music was, despite the critics, very high. When his brother Moss remarked that it seemed to him that Charles was being very conceited to criticize great composers such as Mozart and Wagner because it implied that Charles could write greater music than these men, Charles said, "I don't imply any such thing—I don't have to—I state that it *is* better! Ask any good musician—those who don't agree with me are not good musicians.—"[35]

But Ives had other interests, too. Earlier when he was still at Yale, he had met Harmony Twichell, the beautiful sister of one of his classmates, David C. Twichell. Her father was one of Connecticut's prominent ministers, and Ives as a student had heard him deliver several sermons at Yale's Chapel. The Reverend Joseph Hopkins Twichell, pastor of the Asylum Hill Congregational Church, was part of a famous literary circle centered at Hartford that included John Greenleaf Whittier, Harriet Beecher Stowe, Horace Bushnell, William Dean Howells, and Charles Dudley

Warner. He was also Mark Twain's closest friend and traveling companion in *A Tramp Abroad.*

His daughter Harmony (1876–1969) not only inherited her father's intelligence and interest in literature, but also possessed a quiet kind of beauty and sweetness of temper. She attended Hartford High School and graduated from Miss Porter's School at Farmington in 1896. During the next two years she stayed at home and studied painting with Charles H. Flagg. In 1898 she entered the Hartford Hospital Training School for Nurses and in 1900 was graduated as a registered nurse. Eight years later on June 9, 1908, she married Charles Ives. Both were the same age, thirty-two years old. They had no children of their own, but adopted a child, Edith, in 1910. Edith later (1939) married the New York attorney George Grayson Tyler.[36]

In the meantime Ives was transferred to the Raymond Agency, agents of The Mutual Life Insurance Company. Here he met Julian Myrick, who became Ives' partner in 1907 in the firm of Ives & Myrick. Their firm was extremely successful, ultimately handling millions of dollars worth of business, for they became the largest company in the United States. In 1929 the firm sold forty-nine million dollars worth of insurance, and Charles Ives could have been many times over a millionaire, but he refused to take more money from the business than he needed to keep his family comfortable. He felt strongly that a certain limitation on personal income was desirable, and wrote that he wished a system could be set up whereby each man had a minimum Natural Property Right recognized as his share in majority possessions, with the possibility of working to increase this, up to an agreed maximum. This system, he felt, would combine all the good points of both capitalism and communism.

Because he believed that the current forms of government were ineffective, he constituted a one-man political movement to change things. He formulated a 20th Amendment to the Constitution which was designed to make possible the most direct type of election, with votes taken on issues, not on individuals. Ives felt that the Majority Mind, the law of averages, would be right, and if all people participated in government, they would be able to reconcile the extreme views of minority groups by insisting on all the facts until a solution was evident. *The Majority* was the formal statement of his political beliefs, but he used some of the same ideas in his short story *George's Adventure, or A Study in Money, Coherence, Words, and Other Things: (A Good Model for a Poor Story.)* Another of Ives' political papers, written later, was *Stand By the President and the People.*

Ives' productive period ended with the First World War when a serious physical breakdown resulted in permanent cardiac damage. His complex and sophisticated mind had for some time been under great strain. His long sustained rebellion, and the enormous emotional sensitivity required in retaining and reproducing every single memory had taken their toll for some time. In 1918, at the age of 44, the serious heart attack he suffered forced him to rest for six months and stay away from his business office. After this, his health rapidly deteriorated and he did very little composing for he was in a state of virtual creative paralysis. In 1919-20 he did manage to write a few songs and he started a *Third Pianoforte Sonata.* But there was an increasing tension in Ives that is evident in the ambiguity in his 1922 and 1925 writings. In his concluding remarks on "Some Quarter-tone Impressions" in a music journal in 1925 he said that all he had really written were

> . . . but personal opinions and impressions. How wrong they may seem to me in a few years or hours, I don't like to think, so I'm getting ready to say with the man who went to the horse race: "What I expected didn't happen and I didn't expect it would." [37]

Then in 1927 the tension finally disintegrated his emotional sensitivity and according to his wife, "He came downstairs one day with tears in his eyes and said he couldn't seem to compose any more—nothing went well—nothing sounded right." [38]

After this he seldom went to his insurance office, his business activity slowed down, and in 1930 he announced his retirement from the firm. In 1932, in London, at a concert where Brahms was being played, he noticed for the first time that his perceptions of the high pitches were distorted. Later the same nervous disease that affected his hearing caused trembling in his hands and affected his vision. He could no longer concentrate on music.

Ives' early biographers, Henry and Sidney Cowell, noted that his first breakdown coincided with the First World War in 1917-18. "The war was a shock of the first magnitude to a man whose life was based on his confidence in human progress." [39] David W. Noble, suggesting that the failure of utopian ideals was responsible for destroying many leading thinkers of the Progressive movement, remarked on "the fact that many of the leading thinkers of the Progressive movement were destroyed in effectiveness during the extraordinarily short time of the six years from 1914 to 1920. Men who were leaders in molding public opinion to the outbreak of the War were now, in the post-war years, inarticulate, unable to reach or understand the new generation." [40]

Robert Frame said that along with the other Progressives of his day, Ives had been buoyed up by the evidence he seemed to find everywhere about him in the 1910–1917 period. He thought it would be only a matter of time until all mankind would stand together in harmony and truth, for the miracles of modern industry and technology would usher in a beautiful utopia. Ives was committed to progress, and shattered when World War I brought "a swift and immediate and total smashing of a thought pattern, so that a group of men who before the first World War believed that they were in absolute control of the situation were reduced in six years, from 1914 to 1920, to a frank bewilderment, to an inability to grasp the world around them." [41]

The past tense, which had inhabited Ives' life, could no longer claim significance and urgency. He had the courage to live between the moments of human consciousness that existed between the past and the present, and the courage to "clean house" when he could no longer live in the same way that he had. As he remarked in his *Postface to 114 Songs:* "In fact, gentle borrower, I have not written a book at all—I have merely cleaned house. All that is left is out on the clothes line; but it's good for a man's vanity to have the neighbors see him—on the clothes line." [42]

The *114 Songs* were one of three works Ives had printed at his own expense and distributed free of charge. The others were *The Concord Sonata* and the *Essays Before a Sonata*. Ives thought that the songs and piano sonata were the most accessible to the average person, but the works were extremely difficult, and "the average person" failed him by refusing even to request the free copies. Eventually the ignored volumes reached a few notable people. The Pro-Musica Society founded by French pianist E. Robert Schmitz brought together a number of experimental composers, including Henry Cowell, John Becker, Wallingford Riegger, Carl Ruggles, Otto Luening, and Nicolas Slonimsky, all of whom became friends and proponents of Ives' music. This was the beginning of Ives' recognition.

In 1934 Nicolas Slonimsky made the first recording of an orchestral piece, "Barn Dance" from *Washington's Birthday* and "In the Night" from the *Set for Theatre Orchestra.* But the musical world did not even begin to give Ives the credit and acclaim he deserved until January of 1939 when John Kirkpatrick played the *Concord Sonata* in Town Hall. Still, recognition was slow in coming; America was simply not ready for Ives. Finally, the National Institute of Arts and Letters elected Charles Ives to its membership in 1945. Ives, so long neglected, was then seventy-one years old. He had not yet heard any of his compositions performed by a full orchestra. Then in 1947 Ives received the Pulitzer Prize for *The Third Symphony,* a work he had completed about forty years earlier. The first performance of Ives' *Second Symphony,* composed between 1910 and 1916, had to wait until April 26, 1965 for its first complete performance. But by 1950 major Ives compositions had been played all over the United States, and the critics and the public began to regard the music of Ives highly. Yet the full force of Ives' genius was not recognized until after his death in his eightieth year in 1954,[43] for at this time the "cult" of Ives was only beginning to grow. Today Ives stands, along with Schoenberg, Stravinsky, and Bartok, as one of the outstanding musical geniuses of the twentieth century.

2

IVES AND THE TRANSCENDENTAL TRADITION

A MAN'S CHOICE OF HEROES OFTEN RE-
veals his temperament. Ives' hero was Ralph Waldo Emerson, that
national conscience of America and author of moral aphorisms
for more than a generation. Emerson's high spiritual missions and
idealistic conclusions about life sank deep into an American consciousness that wanted to believe that the world (and particularly
New England) was God's and not the Devil's. Emerson's influence
was ubiquitous and significant. He conceived of American destiny
as a spiritual quest and insisted on the values of the past. Conserving
the old was one means of transcending the present, and Emerson
never apologized for his eclecticism, for his "borrowing" of old
ideas.

Emerson confessedly believed in quotation. He borrowed from
innumerable men and books, and his borrowings found their way
into his prose and verse.[1] "A man will not draw on his invention
when his memory serves him with a word as good," Emerson wrote.
There is no dishonor in mental indebtedness, but as he said in
his essay *Quotation and Originality,* he borrowed "proudly, royally,
as a king borrows from one of his attendants the coin that bears
his own image and superscription."[2] Such convictions were natural,
for Emerson had a synthetic mind; his world was processed by
abstraction, with similarities seen everywhere. Nor did he clarify
past truths of inherent limitations with further explanations. Emerson was doubtful about the certainty of man's knowledge of particulars; he thought that the physical world was the creation of mind.
"The perception of identity unites all things and explains one by

another," he wrote in his explanation of the poem *The Sphinx,* "and the most rare and strange is equally facile as the most common. But if the mind live only in particulars, and see only differences (wanting the power to see the whole—all in each) then the world addresses to this mind a question it cannot answer, and each new fact tears it in pieces, and it is vanquished by the distracting variety." [3]

The mysterious contradiction involved in such convictions is the result chiefly of a belief that it is not the thing, but the way the thing is said that matters. All things are metaphors, and facts turn out to correspond to spiritual laws. This conception characterized life as a creative process of burgeoning and fertility. "We can point nowhere," remarked Emerson, "to anything final; but tendency appears on all hands: planet, system, constellation, total nature is growing like a field of maize in July; is becoming somewhat else, is in rapid metamorphosis." [4] Organic productivity meant that substance was really process.

In all this Charles Ives found sustenance for his life and work, for Ives, as he himself said in *Essays Before a Sonata,* was a Transcendentalist. Ives' Transcendentalism is well known, and such eminent music critics as Wilfrid Mellers and Gilbert Chase have studied and written about it. [5] My purpose is to show how his Transcendentalism opened the gates to—not divinity—but the subconscious and a stream-of-consciousness technique. Moreover, a look at Emerson's life shows that Ives may have patterned his own life-style after the great philosopher, a theory that might help to clarify a number of contradictions in Ives' life and work.

Many biographies and articles give us vivid personal details about Emerson's life. In spite of his dictum that "whoso would be a man must be a nonconformist," Emerson was a strict conformist in his social and family relations. He strictly observed the social forms, including his role in his home town. He had the good taste of the gentleman and was deferential toward others; he also took a leading part in all civic activities, participating in such rousing activities as dedicating local cemeteries, and serving on the library board and the school board. But his courage ran out with his ink, for to him innovations in conventions or family morality were equally unthinkable. As an overseer of Harvard he once cast the decisive vote in continuing to make attendance at College Chapel compulsory. One might have expected otherwise from the author of the *Divinity School Address,* yet even after he resigned from the Unitarian pulpit, he continued to preach most Sundays through 1838 in various churches. Nor did he mind his wife and children attending church regularly and contributing to the plate. He must have been difficult to live with, for he made it quite plain that he considered it his duty to be meticulous in all his obligations as a husband and father. He believed that feelings should be channeled and controlled within the context of the family, which to him was sacred.[6]

Frank Rossiter makes it quite plain that Ives was deeply committed to the genteel, middle-class life of his time and social class.[7] This commitment, which he acquired from his family background, became even stronger after he married Harmony Twichell in 1908. The daily rounds of his existence show him to be a part of the same "genteel tradition" that Emerson propounded. And like Emerson, his life became a long series of ceremonial gestures against the very gentility that he was supporting in his daily life. "These gestures were safe," remarks Rossiter, "in that they offered no real threat to middle-class gentility—but they gave him the feeling that he was rebelling against that gentility.[8]

Ives' use of the past was related to the major beliefs and attitudes of the Transcendentalists, for he shared common qualities with the Transcendentalists of another generation. George Santayana, philosopher and writer, calls Transcendentalism "systematic subjectivism" which studies the perspectives of knowledge as they radiate from the self. Transcendentalism, he says, is "a plan of those avenues of inference by which our ideas of things must be reached, if they are to afford any systematic or distant vistas." [9]

The Transcendentalists regarded the realities of the finite universal merely as symbols of an underlying, immaterial and immanent essence. This "essence", shared by God, man, and nature, meant that all things were interrelated. These moral and philosophical truths could be flushed from the symbolic bushes of natural phenomena by studying Nature. The intrepid hunter of such malleable moral precepts would find that the Transcendental tracks led backward to European thought, German Romanticism, and ultimately Oriental mysticism.

As a group, the early Transcendentalists were critical, restless, sensitive, and highly sophisticated. They were Utopians seriously reacting to radical social changes, and were very articulate liberals, independent in opinion. Music was important to them as an expression of their beliefs, and although they produced no significant musical figures, except the critic John Sullivan Dwight, their ideas on music greatly influenced the development of Ives' musical thought.

A distinguishing characteristic of Ives' music, for example, is his use of popular songs, hymns, and the like, music which the world of acclaimed artists and renowned composers often despised. (See. Ex. 1, 2) That his Transcendentalist hero Thoreau centered

EXAMPLE 1. Ives, *Second Pianoforte Sonata,* "Concord." Copyright by Associated Music Publishers. Used by permission. P. 32, measures 2, 3, 4. The second movement, "Hawthorne" shows Ives' use of the revival hymn "Jesus, Lover of My Soul."

EXAMPLE 2. Ives, *Second Piano Sonata,* "Concord". Copyright by Associated Music Publishers. Used by permission. P. 34, measures 7, 8, 9, 10, 11. The second movement, "Hawthorne" shows a borrowed circus march.

his interest almost exclusively on the popular and sentimental ballads of the day seems no coincidence.[10] Nor was he the only Transcendentalist who liked the humbler, more natural and popular form of musical expression. C. P. Cranch liked popular music and Margaret Fuller was interested in all music, including American Indian songs and chants.

Aside from this choice of type of musical expression, Ives' belief in what constitutes music traces directly back to Thoreau. (See Ex. 3) Ives once remarked, "My God! What has sound got to do

Thoreau
Adapted from themes in a Second Pianoforte Sonata

EXAMPLE 3. Ives, "Thoreau". Copyright 1933, Merion Music. Used by permission of the publisher. Note the lack of barlines and key signature, the informal speech style, and the realistic details such as "bell" sounds. The piano accompaniment at the point where the text reads "rapt in revery" corresponds to p. 64, the first line of The Concord Sonata ("Thoreau", Movement IV).

with music!," a cryptic remark that many thought placed him in the avant-garde.[11] But it was Thoreau who first expanded the definition of "music" beyond the strictly formal and technical sense of matters of harmony, counterpoint, rhythm, or instrumentation. He used the word in a catholic and encyclopedic sense so that sound and silence are construed as forms of music. "What is this music?" he wrote in his *Journal.* "Why, thinner and more evanescent than ether; subtler than sound, for it is only a disposition of sound. It is to sound what color is to matter. It is the color of a flame, or of a rainbow, or of water. Only one sense has known it. The least profitable, the least tangible fact, which cannot be bought or cultivated but by virtuous methods, and yet our ears ring with it like shells left on the shore." [12] Thoreau thought silence was musical, and sound itself an utterance of silence. "Silence has no end; speech is but the beginning of it," he wrote in another entry in the *Journals.* [13]

Daniel E. Rider quotes a letter from Thoreau to his friend, Harrison Gray Otis Blake (August 8, 1854) [14] which further clarifies Thoreau's opinion on the relationship between silence and sound. Thoreau is describing a boat trip up the river to Fair Haven Pond:

> The falling dews seemed to strain and purify the air and I was soothed with an infinite stillness. . . . Vast hollows of silence stretched away in every side, and my being expanded in proportion, and filled them. Then first could I appreciate sound, and find it musical.[15]

Thoreau thought that there were specific qualities intrinsic in sound that could be classed as musical, and that if a person's ears were "clear and unprejudiced" he could detect the finest music. The music of nature interested him more than the music of man. "One will lose no music by not attending oratorios and operas," he wrote. "I get my new experiences still, not at the opera listening to the Swedish Nightingale, but at Beck Stow's Swamp listening to the native wood thrush." [16]

Telegraph lines, first strung through Concord in August 1851, gave Thoreau a new musical interest. To his intense delight, he discovered that the telegraph wires made a gigantic aeolian harp. "I put my ear to one of the posts," he said, "And it seemed to me as if every pore of the wood was filled with music, labored with the strain,—as if every fiber was affected and being seasoned or timed, rearranged according to a new and more harmonious law." [17]

Thoreau's close associate Emerson revealed some interest in the theoretical and aesthetic nature of music; certainly he was acquainted with the theories pertaining to the organic form in music, and it is probable that John Sullivan Dwight influenced his ideas regarding the aesthetics of music. Emerson acknowledged music's power of communication and he sometimes spoke of the religious and spiritual significance of music.[18] Accordingly, he wrote "Concord Hymn to be sung to the tune of "Old Hundred" " at the dedication of a monument at Old North Bridge in Concord on July 4, 1837. One of the choir members who sang Emerson's hymn was Henry David Thoreau.

Like Emerson, Margaret Fuller was most interested in the psychological impact of music. This interest in the psychological aspect of music is a distinguishing feature of the Transcendental impact on an art form. Fuller, like Emerson and Thoreau, was concerned with her own thought and emotional processes upon hearing music rather than in the music itself. Self-knowledge through an aesthetic experience promised personal triumph or "transcendence" to fulfillment, and as such reflected the idealism and optimism of Transcendentalism. Upon hearing Beethoven (who was, incidentally, a hero for all Transcendentalists and also for Ives) Margaret Fuller wrote:

> This is the dart within the heart, as well as I can tell it:—At moments, the music of the universe, which daily I am upheld by hearing, seems to stop. I fall like a bird when the sun is eclipsed, not looking for such darkness. . . . Only by emotion do we know thee, Nature. To lean upon thy heart, and feel its pulses vibrate to our own;—that is knowledge, for that is love, the love of infinite beauty, of infinite love. Thought will never make us be born again. . . .[19]

Like the other Transcendentalists, she thought that music was capable of pointing out great truths such as "all is in each and each in all." Like most Transcendentalists she filled in all the blanks and extended her thought at the beginning, middle, and end, so that it finally became a universal vision in which all truth was comprised in music and mathematics. For Margaret Fuller, music was a groove into human experience that today lies in the realm of the psychologist. She used musical analogues to describe various degrees of individual growth or of unusual compatibility or understanding between individuals.[20]

This psychological interest in music was carried a step further by Transcendental music critic John Sullivan Dwight in an essay entitled "The Influence of Music on the Intellectual Powers." Writing apparently under the influence of Kant and Coleridge, he breaks down his analysis of music's influence on the mind by classifying the activities of the mind into the imagination, understanding and memory, and then demonstrating how music affects each separate function of the mind.[21] The original stimulus of the music makes an impression on the emotions, but it is the power of the imagination that calls up various images, according to Dwight. These vague images assume shape as the music fulfills its potential in theme and motif. Time and again in his criticism he refers to music as "the language of the sentiments" which appeals to the emotions. Another one of his themes is that of music's intrinsic relationship with nature. In both themes one can discern the pattern of Dwight's aesthetics: from music's origin in nature to music as a universal language to music as the arch reformer.[22] "Music is a universal language, subtly penetrating all the walls of time and space," he wrote.[23] In his remarks on the role of music in stimulating the mind to make associations, Dwight hit upon the stream-of-consciousness conception. Every feeling awakened by music in turn awakened many other images and memories in minds.

> Here the material part, which is measured sound, is the embodiment and sensible representative, as well as the re-acting cause, of that which we call impulse, and sentiment, feeling, the spring of all our action and expression. . . .[24]

Music thus acts directly upon the memory as the listener attempts to retain certain melodies which conjure up the most images.

George William Curtis was still another Transcendentalist who believed that music's primary appeal is to the heart, not the mind. He regarded music as a unique form of communication whose meaning was indefinite, impressionistic and incomplete. Although he believed that music could not be defined, his own writing has been compared to music.[25] For him, music is "the universal interpreter," the art that possesses "the gift of tongues." It is universal primarily in the Transcendental sense that all the universe, all parts of it, are made of one unified substance.[26] As such, music was but an aspect of the Transcendentalists' metaphysics of an essence that supports life and nature.[27]

For Curtis, music's role was to shadow the deeper mysteries and secrets of Nature, to deal in impressions and images rather than in ideas. He thought that the typical state that music should invoke for the listener could best be described as a trance or a reverie.[28] Curtis' insistence upon the emotions as the key to music is a reflection of the larger Transcendental movement, for all the Transcendentalists who mentioned music equated it with the emotions. Dwight, of course, was far more explicit and exhaustive in his analysis and paid more attention to the role of the intellect; Margaret Fuller was concerned indirectly through the psychological base of the emotions with the issue.

What these particular Transcendentalists illustrate with all their talk of "music as emotion" is a shift in ways of thinking from objective modes to subjective. Music (a synonym for life) was beginning to be seen as a means of communicating with one's own thoughts, as primarily a flux and a becoming. This reassertion of the Heraclitean doctrine of the Flowing can be traced to Emerson's Over-Soul, which is compared to water no less than a dozen times in his essay. Emerson saw himself standing on the bank of a river watching the endless current upon which floated past him objects of all shapes and colors. Such recurrent images of flowing and water were the special signatures of nineteenth-century poets—Wordsworth, Arnold, Whitman. Yet it is Emerson's world that concerns us, a world in which nothing is left secure because it has been infiltrated and dissolved by thought. His images of flowing culminated in a paragraph of his *Lecture on the Times* (1841):

> The main interest which any aspects of the Times can have for us, is the great spirit which gazes through them, the light which they can shed on the wonderful questions, What we are? and Whither we tend? We do not wish to be deceived. Here we drift, like white sails across the wild ocean, now bright on the wave, now darkling in the trough of the sea;—but from what port did we sail? Who knows? Or to what port are we bound? Who knows! There is no one to tell us but such poor weather-tossed mariners as ourselves, whom we speak as we pass, or who have hoisted some signal or floated to us some letter in a bottle from far. But what know they more than we? They also found themselves on this wondrous sea. No; from the older sailors, nothing. Over all their speaking-trumpets,

the gray sea and the loud winds answer, Not in us: not in Time. . . .[29]

Not too surprisingly we find Ives also obsessed with water. No one can read through his *Essays Before a Sonata* without noting the fluid moments. He also seems more than a little fond of quoting tunes with watery references—"Columbia, the Gem of the Ocean,"

A Farewell to Land

EXAMPLE 4. Ives. "A Farewell to Land." Copyright 1935, by Merion Music, Inc. Used by permission of the publisher. "A Farewell to Land" also uses water-imagery. Note the use of 12-tone technique and polytonality.

"Throw Out the Life Line," "Shall we Gather at the River?", "My Bonnie Lies Over the Ocean," even the "Irish Washerwoman." "General William Booth Enters Heaven" repeatedly "washed in the Blood of the Lamb." "A Farewell to Land" is just that, for the sea takes over in the second line. (See Ex. 4) Other water-songs include "At Sea," "The White Gulls," "From the Incantation," "Premonitions," "At the River," "The Swimmers," and "The New River" and literally dozens of others that either mention water, streams, rivers or floating or have some covert reference such as "Events that drift past."

A perfect example of water-images and their meaning musically is the song *Tom Sails Away*. (See Ex. 5) The words are Ives'

EXAMPLE 5. Ives' "Tom Sails Away." Copyright 1935, Merion Music, Inc. Used by permission of the publisher.

own and deal with an experience viewed retrospectively. The texture is amorphous, the melody without metrical accent, and gradually chords dissolve into free polyrhythm and polyharmony. It is a metreless kind of musical impressionism reminding us of the flow of time.

Another image of the flow of time is the third movement of the *Three Places in New England*, "the Housatonic at Stockbridge"— described by Ives as "A Sunday morning walk that Mrs. Ives and I took near Stockbridge the summer after we were married. We walked in the meadows along the River and heard the distant singing from the Church across the River. The mist had not entirely left the river bed, and the colours, the running water, the banks and the trees were something that one would always remember." Naturally, water-images abound. Without remarking on the idea of flow, Wilfrid Mellers describes the piece beautifully as a personal reminiscence that suggests both the chapel singing that Ives heard floating over the water through the mist and the tranquil security of the love between himself and his wife. The melody, absorbed in a haze of strings, is countered by "sounds of Nature—of river, mist, and rustling leaves." Finally the melody is engulfed by these sounds, and "suspended, unresolved on a sigh." According to Mellers, the piece with great poignancy reveals both "the centrality of human love and also its impermanence in the non-human contest of the natural world." [30] At this point few could resist quoting Sigmund Freud, "It is fair to say that there is no group of ideas that is incapable of representing sexual facts and wishes." [31] The Freudian interpreter would, of course, define anything liquid as female. While the psychoanalytic meaning of music is decidedly material of undetermined fiber content, Ives himself made it explicit how he had grown aware of other meanings of meaning beyond mere sense:

> Do all inspirational images, states, conditions, or whatever they may be truly called, have for a dominant part, if not for a source, some actual experience in life or of the social relation? To think that they do not—always at least—would be a relief. But as we are trying to consider music made and heard by human beings (and not by birds or angels), it seems difficult to suppose that even subconscious images can be separated from some human experience; there must be something behind subconsciousness to produce consciousness, and so on. [32]

Bentley Layton in *An Introduction to the 114 Songs of Charles Ives* remarks that "The use of subconscious and partly conscious levels of perception similar to that of the *Unanswered Question* occurs in many other works and passages in Ives' music." He cites as examples *The Housatonic* and *The Pond*. [33] Something like this feeling was the usual result of the Transcendental conception that the idea is always greater than any expression of it. The recurring idea of water, the permanence of the sea—our first mother—gives further evidence of Nature's constant and transcendent laws. This constancy, a kind of dawning of elemental consciousness, indicates that the soul—a part of the Over-Soul—endures or transcends.

The use of water-imagery also indicates a change in the prevailing concepts of the mind. While men of the eighteenth century spoke of the mind as a passive receptacle, a mirror, a tabula rasa, or a wax plate on which impressions stamp themselves, men of the nineteenth century spoke of it as an active agent—as a wind-harp, a stream, a lamp, or a growing plant. The stream, wind-harp, and growing plant are analogies common to Emerson, Thoreau, Whitman, and Melville.[34] The sharp transitions between various states of objectivity had given way to a transitionless subjectivity.

This shift to the inner man constitutes the first element of Transcendentalism in an art form. The second element is best expressed in the negative and is a direct result of the first. It is a lack of structure. The problem of Transcendentalism in an art form was to demonstrate unity beneath all manner of variety. The whole philosophy embodied in each piece led toward sameness and diversity, standardization and anarchy, radicalism and restraint. Like Shiva with his eight arms, the formula was abstraction instanced by numerous embodiments. Lacking transitions, nothing is constructed as a whole. Emerson summed it up when he confessed to Carlyle in 1838 that his paragraphs were only collections of "infinitely repellent particles."

These same repellent particles are evoked in "General Putnam's Camp," from the *Three Places in New England*, where several military and rag-time tunes are played together in different keys, different rhythms, and different tempi accompanied by rhythmic nonmusic, representing perhaps the shuffling of the crowd. All is present at once; the flux of life and chaos is part of the music in an attempt to describe unity within chaos.

Ives' concern with the problem of imposing the Unity of the Over-Soul on the chaos of experience led him to seek resolution in the sonata form as a principle of composition. It was a means, so to speak, of having his cake and eating it, too. Within a very old form he could experience the kind of organic growth and lack of repetitions that constituted Nature. Yet as the revival preacher admonished his congregation: "Walkin' through a watermelon patch don't make you a watermelon." So a stroll through the sonata form doesn't make a sonata, and the form and substance of *The Concord Sonata* does not justify calling the piece a sonata. And, in fact, Ives did not at first intend to write a sonata. According to a letter from Charles Ives to John Kirkpatrick (West Redding, Conn., October 11, 1935) the Emerson movement of *The Concord Sonata* started out to be an overture with piano, but it was never

fully scored. Further, Ives wrote, the music should have some of
Emerson's freedom in action and thought, as Emerson seldom gave
any of his lectures in exactly the same way, and the published
essays were not kept to literally. Ives said that he remembered
his grandmother saying that when she heard Emerson lecture on
the New England Reformers in the 1850's, she was startled to find
that the printed text was hardly more than an outline of his lecture.

The *Concord Sonata* (see Ex. 6) begins with a large, complex,
barless period with the motive stated in octaves in the bass con-

I. "Emerson"

EXAMPLE 6. Ives. *Second Pianoforte Sonata.* I. "Emerson". Copyright by
Associated Music Publishers. Used by permission. P. 1, mea-
sures 1, 3. Measure 3 illustrates Ives' use of the motif from
Beethoven's *Fifth Symphony.*

founded by a polyphony of chords in the widest possible tonal range forming dissonant counterpoints and free-rhythm. The piece is perpetually evolving: themes change their identities and are absorbed into a continuous texture. The epic forces (exemplified by the motif from Beethoven's *Fifth Symphony*) conflict with the individual verse sections which are barred and comparatively simple. The movement simply disintegrates at the end, for Ives' philosophy was that nothing is ever complete.

Ives interprets his sonata as both impressionistic and transcendental in his notes:

> The reading-matter throughout is taken from the composer's "Essays Before a Sonata" written primarily as a preface or reason for this (second pianoforte) Sonata—"Concord, Mass., 1804–60" a group of four pieces, called a sonata for want of a more exact name, as the form, perhaps substance, does not justify it. The music and prefaces were intended to be printed together, but as it was found that this would make a cumbersome volume they are separate. The whole is an attempt to present (one person's) impression of the spirit of transcendentalism that is associated in the minds of many with Concord, Mass., of over a half century ago. This is undertaken in impressionistic pictures of Emerson and Thoreau, a sketch of the Alcotts, and a scherzo supposed to reflect a lighter quality which is often found in the fantastic side of Hawthorne. The first and last movements do not aim to give any programs of the life or of any particular work of either Emerson or Thoreau but rather composite pictures or impressions. They are, however, so general in outline that, from some viewpoints, they may be as far from accepted impressions (from true conceptions, for that matter) as the valuation which they purport to be of the influence of the life, thought, and character of Emerson and Thoreau is inadequate.[35]

In this piece, Ives' use of the term "sonata" is close to the way the term was used in the sixteenth and early seventeenth centuries for almost any kind of instrumental composition, implying nothing about form.[36] Ives has thought about form and thinks that coherence, to a certain extent, must bear some relation to the listener's subconscious perspective.[37] He gives the example of the critic who listens to thousands of concerts a year and hears the same formal relations of tones, cadences, progressions and so on, so that finally instead of listening *to* music he listens *around* it. "And from this subconscious viewpoint, he inclines perhaps more to the thinking *about* than thinking *in* music," Ives writes.[38] He then suggests that if the critic could go into some other line of business for a year or so, his perspective would be more naturally normal.

Apparently, Ives' view, which found its justification in program music, was that each composition creates not only its own inner form (form within; e.g., tones, intervals, scales, tonality, consonance, dissonance, meter, rhythm, phrase, theme, and all other devices) but also its outer structure (form *of* composition; e.g., certain schemes which govern the structure-at-large, the plan of construction, often traditional, as the fugue or sonata).[39]

Ives' remark that "The unity of a sonata movement has long been associated with its form, and to a greater extent than is necessary," [40] predates the widespread tendency among modern composers and writers to deny, or at least to minimize the importance of musical forms.[41] Ives may also have misused or ignored classical forms in his attempt to create a series of musical *Gestalten*. In his songs, for example, Ives seldom uses the familiar ABA form (simple ternary form), but instead creates one little musical "vignette" and then moves on to a new one, almost never repeating himself except perhaps in a rhythm. Thus his structure is largely additive, one musical idea provoking another, and so forth, until the end of the song is reached. His imitation of life is often conveyed through instability; the animal's pacing in *In the Cage* is suggested by a nontonal, chromatic vocal line while the small cage is a repeated set of chords founded on fourths. This is a kind of literal imitation based on a reminiscence: Ives' memory of a little boy watching a caged animal, restless and frustrated, pacing up and down. And the little boy wondered "Is life anything like that?" Thus the song becomes a psychological experience, and in its incompleteness, a rejection of European classical song-form, which would by its nature, require a sense of completion.

The lack of traditional structure (see Ex. 7) in Ives' music may also have been his reaction against the strict conformity of his education at Yale. Certainly the training at the hands of Horatio Parker, an imposing authoritarian figure in the German academic tradition, would have been reason enough for revolt to a free-wheeling spirit. Yet the lack of structure in Ives' form was a natural product of the cleavage between his two lives. The cleavage between his world of the spirit, of Transcendental past, and the rapidly changing society of an industrial revolution created an impassable contradiction. Consequently, his exaltation of content over form

EXAMPLE 7. Ives. *Second Pianoforte Sonata.* "Concord". Movement I, "Emerson", p. 5. Copyright by Associated Music Publishers. Used by permission. Although *The Concord Sonata* does not follow typical sonata form, Ives bases his unity on a series of aspects of a subject. As this example shows, parts of the music are associated with poetry and others with prose.

anticipated the declaration of the Chicago architects that "form follows function." Louis Sullivan's celebrated dictum of form and function emerged from Transcendental arguments about the functional basis for aesthetics. Horatio Greenough's theories of structure may have started it all, and his discussions with Emerson influenced the Concord sage's ideas.[42] "Fitness is so inseparable an accompaniment of beauty, that it has been taken for it," wrote Emerson.[43] Thoreau also thought that beauty developed within, "and whatever additional beauty of this kind is destined to be produced will be preceded by a like unconscious beauty of life." [44] The idea that art could grow organically with the "heart" as nucleus was in the air.

Moreover, the kind of borrowing that Ives considered necessary for his art did not lead to a tightly structured form, which he undoubtedly could see from the outset. But it was Emerson who first summed it up: "What you owe to me—you will vary the phrase—but I shall still recognize my thought. But what you say from the same idea, will have to me also the expected unexpectedness which belongs to every new work of Nature." [45] Ives, of course, says it a little more neatly when he remarks that "What I expected didn't happen and I didn't expect it would." [46]

The shift to the subjective, to the inner man, and the corresponding lack of structure caused many to think of the influence of Transcendental thought as an influence of vapid inanities and soggy emotionalism. Trying to fit the raw realism, corny tunes, and so on that Ives used into the same picture of Ives as Transcendentalist gave one a sense of oddity, of incongruity. So a good many people shrugged and labeled him a primitive or an eccentric, or at best, a pioneer with freakish courage. But in writing the strong accents of daily talk, Ives was no pioneer. The rediscovery of the common was a fundamental element of Transcendental writers. "I embrace the common," said Emerson, "I explore and sit at the feet of the familiar, the low. . . ." [47] Emerson, often buried under abstraction, was increasingly aware of the need to break through the conventional style of writing to the language of conversation. He wrote in his *Journal* in 1840 that:

> The language of the street is always strong. What can describe the folly and emptiness of scolding like the word jawing? I feel too the force of the double negative, though clean contrary to our grammar rules. And I confess to some pleasure from the stinging rhetoric of a rattling oath in the mouth of truckmen and teamsters. How laconic and brisk it is by the side of a page of the North

American Review. Cut these words and they would bleed; they
are vascular and alive; they walk and run. Moreover, they who
speak them have this elegancy, that they do not trip in their speech.
It is a shower of bullets, whilst Cambridge men and Yale men correct
themselves and begin again at every half sentence.[48]

The effort at accuracy in the description of human behavior,
including the transcription of colloquial speech, was undoubtedly
of primary importance to Ives as it was to his Transcendental
counterparts. "Charlie Rutlage," "General William Booth Enters
Heaven," and "Nov. 2, 1920" plunge right in with immediate
impact. Just as in realistic literature, we learn about the speaker
through his words or through unstructured interior monologue.
The artificiality of the singer is gone, and so is the nineteenth
century "hero". The power of Ives' colloquial speech rests on its
typicality of the common man.

In "General William Booth Enters Heaven" Ives uses chaos
as part of the music to build up to a great climax of religious
frenzy to render incarnate the hot-gospeller's situation. The piece
begins with the piano imitating a drum (the gospeller's march tune)
and through cluster-chords adding the noises of the crowd. The
piano lurches forward ("Walking lepers followed rank on rank");
the drum beats in octaves (often misplaced from the belligerent
rhetoric of the preacher), and the hysterical pattern of marcato
accents and tonal meanderings leads the singer, bellowing off-key
to a number of emotional climaxes ("Unwashed legions with the
ways of Death"—and "Death" receives a big sFz for punctuation).
This strident climax abruptly changes to a lyrical reiteration of
the question, "Are you washed in the Blood of the Lamb?" Each
time the grotesque horror-comedy of tent-revivalism is intensified
as Ives moves the pitch upward and changes tempo; the syncopa-
tions become more savage and jerky and the "hallelujah!" is a
din of independent voices "barking up Jesus."

In a particularly interesting passage of this song, the singer
illustrates the text ("Booth saw not, but led his queer ones, Round
and round—round and round and round and round and round
and round and round and round and round") by circling vocally
"round and round" on a three-note figure. In the accompaniment,
the pianist "circles" on a two-note figure underscored with references to the revival hymn tune *Cleansing Fountain* which begins
"There is a fountain filled with blood." (See Ex. 8)

EXAMPLE 8. Ives, "General William Booth Enters Heaven." Copyright
1935, Merion Music, Inc. Used by permission. Measures
85–91. Circled notes point out Ives' use of the revival hymn
"Cleansing Fountain."

Ives builds "General William Booth Enters Heaven" on rami-
fications of Lowell Mason's revival hymn "There is a Fountain"
(also called "Cleansing Fountain"). (See Ex. 9) Ives not only quotes
the hymn literally, as in the Adagio section ("Jesus came from
the courthouse door" . . .) in the key of A♭, but the sections
"Are you washed in the Blood of the Lamb?" are derivations of
the hymn. (See Exs. 10 and 11)

The realism inherent in this piece is apparent in Ives' use
of vernacular materials. He himself described it as "a study in
sevenths and other things" and also as "a parody of the Yankee
drawl." His use of every kind of musical technique and sound
that seemed to him to be appropriate—whether European Romantic harmonies, traditional Protestant hymnody, popular sentimental
"trite" formulas or borrowed tunes, or simply noisy sounds—illustrates the same kind of rediscovery of the common that Emerson
talked about, but never used himself.

This realism is not based on the "spectator" theory of experience but on the consciousness of man's involvement actively in
a moving world of action and reaction. Ives interpreted the everyday
world as a diversity of means for carrying out a unitary purpose
that was situated in an ultimate realm beyond the here-and-now.
The world's variety of things was thus a transcendental unifier
that infused them all with its single spirit. By this mode of interpretation all the world became viewed as a set of instrumentalities.[49]

There Is a Fountain Filled with Blood

EXAMPLE 9. Lowell Mason, "There is a Fountain." Public domain.

EXAMPLE 10. Ives. "General William Booth Enters Heaven." Copyright 1935, Merion Music, Inc. Used by permission of the publisher. Measure 82–84.

EXAMPLE 11. Ives. "General William Booth Enters Heaven". Copyright 1935, Merion Music, Inc. Used by permission of the publisher. Measures 4–6.

Transcendentalism thus divided into two streams. The first was active, scientific and pragmatic. The second was passive, mystical, and psychological. But Ives was never conscious of the dichotomy, for he possessed the past not only through his mind but as an experienced musical discipline. Therefore he inevitably possessed a concrete present as well, for "reality," as Emerson once remarked, "has a sliding floor." [50]

3

THE STREAM OF CONSCIOUSNESS IN IVES' WORKS

T RANSCENDENTALISM PAVED THE WAY for the doctrine of the subconscious. A lingering Transcendental belief in the living qualities of matter inclined some New England physicians to a special interest in the powers of the mind. Hypnotism, suggestion and the mental healers that flourished in the late nineteenth century seemed to offer evidence for the potency of thoughts and emotions.[1] Indeed, innumerable articles and books on the doctrine of the potency of the subconscious or unconscious appeared before Freud's view of the unconscious became known. Americans knew of the subconscious chiefly from medical men such as Pierre Janet or Morton Prince, or from philosophers such as Johann Friedrich Herbart, Arthur Schopenhauer, and Karl Robert Eduard von Hartmann. The beliefs filtered down (or up, as the case may be) to researchers in psychic communication such as F.W.H. Myers and Edmund Gurney, and to the ubiquitous mind-cure specialists such as Lydia Pinkham who had such eminent patients as William James.

The intellectual opinion of the day was stated in many literary and mystical accounts of the subconscious or unconscious mind. A random example was John Edward Maude, whose account in 1882 of "The Unconscious in Education" stated that some ideas were conscious and that some, such as general impressions and faint sensations outside of conscious attention, were unconscious, but no idea or sensation was ever forgotten whether or not it was recalled to consciousness.[2] Americans were thus accustomed to reading and hearing phrases such as "the unconscious, underlying forces of human society." [3]

By 1898 Morton Prince had discovered that the baffling tangle of the neuroses could be charted. After a searching inquiry into every detail of the origin, history and character of the symptoms, he wrote that "how often what seems to be a mere chaos of unrelated mental and physical phenomena will resolve itself into a series of logical events." [4] Associations, Prince later taught, were best thought of as aspects of neurological habit. The repetition of "ideas, sensations, emotions, and organic physiological processes" together caused a tendency for each element to excite all the others."[5]

The "mystical wave" brought on by Transcendental beliefs became a public craze for mind cures by 1906. This same "mystical wave" that was producing occultism and symbolism in art, music, literature and the drama, was, as Frances X. Dercum insisted, the genesis of psychoanalysis as an idea in America. What Dercum did was to identify the mind-cure fad with the new movements of intellectual and artistic rebellion after 1912. In fact, many of the same people were involved in both.[6] A significant number of writers in the Progressive era turned away from naturalism and material realism and sought instead psychological realism. Many were profoundly influenced by what Arthur O. Lovejoy called a "radical and romantic turn in evolutionary thought that spread to America around 1909." [7] Henri Bergson replaced Herbert Spencer as the public idol, and some religious liberals thought that his Life Force might be a new scientific revelation of the nature of God. Bergson's *Creative Evolution* taught that energy could manifest itself in sudden mutations without orderly progression from previous forms, an idea that reinforced intuition and spontaneity. The intellectually fashionable Bergson attracted limousines and Carl Jung to his lectures at Columbia University in 1911. Jung proceeded to adopt Bergson's Life Force.[8] Jung started with an assumption that emotion or "affectivity" was the determinant of all psychological life, of every thought and of every action. His second assumption was that sensations, ideas, and the effects connected with these were grouped together in consciousness as entities or "molecules" as he called them. So every memory, with its accompanying emotion made up such a unit, or "affective complex." [9]

The constellation of opinions and attitudes towards the subconscious grew and a few daring innovators developed a hopeful psychological approach to nervous and mental disorder between 1885–1909. They found that some kinds of nervous and mental illness could result from patterns of association, formed on a subconscious level. In 1885 Morton Prince published that "mystery of mysteries", the relation of mind to brain. The *Nature of Mind and Human Automatism* advanced two principles: (1) the influence of thought, emotion and will, and (2) the organization of ideas in habitual trains of association. He called the latter a commonplace and "self-evident" assumption of nineteenth century psychology.[10] Each thought was determined by a preceding one, and ideas were linked in complex chains of associations. Prince believed that this theory explained every phenomenon from the simplest muscular movement to reveries, dreams, or the creative activity of a Coleridge or a Mozart, which seemed to occur in both artists as a kind of spontaneous, almost automatic activity.[11]

The discovery that memories, thoughts, and feelings existed outside the primary consciousness constituted a great step forward in psychology. The application of this concept to works of art (at first fiction) resulted in a distinct approach, an approach called "stream-of-consciousness," a term first coined by William James.[12] Consciousness indicated the entire area of mental attention, from preconsciousness on through the levels of the mind up to and including the highest one of rational communicable awareness.[13] Stream-of-consciousness works are thus concerned with the whole level of mental processes. The higher level, the level of memories, often flows in a kind of order and can be represented by verbal communication. The lower levels are not rationally controlled, or logically ordered, but constitute a kind of mental awareness. Consciousness, then, is a catch-all term for everything: sensations, memories, feelings, conceptions, fancies, whims, intuitions, visions, and imaginations. Thus, as Robert Humphrey remarks, we may, on inductive grounds, conclude that the realm of life with which the stream-of-consciousness is concerned is mental and spiritual experience—both the "whatness" and the "howness" of it. The whatness includes the categories of mental experiences—sensations, memories, imaginations, conceptions, and intuitions. The howness includes the symbolizations, the feelings, and the processes of association.[14] Sometimes, of course, it is impossible to separate the what from the how, as in the case of a memory which is both part of mental content and also a mental process.

The attempt to create human consciousness in music is likewise an attempt to deal with the "what" and the "how." For example, Henry Bellamann's program notes of 1927, based on conversations with Ives, describe the overall plan of the Fourth Symphony:

> This symphony . . . consists of four movements—a prelude, a majestic fugue, a third movement in a comedy vein, and a finale of transcendental spiritual content. The aesthetic program of the work is . . . the searching questions of What? and Why? which the spirit of man asks of life. This is particularly the sense of the prelude. The three succeeding movements are the diverse answers in which existence replies . . . the fugue . . . is an expression of the reaction of life into formalism and ritualism. The succeeding movement . . . is not a scherzo. . . . It is a comedy in the sense that Hawthorne's *Celestial Railroad* is comedy. Indeed this work of Hawthorne's may be considered as a sort of incidental program in which an exciting, easy, and worldly progress through life is contrasted with the trials of the Pilgrims in their journey through the swamp. The occasional slow episodes—Pilgrims' hymns—are constantly crowded out and overwhelmed by the former. The dream, or fantasy, ends with an interruption of reality—The Fourth of July in Concord—brass bands, drum corps, etc. . . .[15]

In the New Music printing of *The Fourth Symphony* of 1929, Ives ascribes to Bellamann's note a further sentence: "The last movement is an apotheosis of the preceding content, in terms that have something to do with the reality of existence and its religious experience."

It is a psychical autobiography, then, and in fact, the *Fourth Symphony* combines elements from many of Ives' earlier pieces. For example, the third movement, *Fugue: Andante Moderato*, is a double fugue on Lowell Mason's *Missionary Hymn* "From Greenland's Icy Mountains. . ." and Oliver Holden's *Coronation* "All hail the power of Jesus' name . . ." (the countersubject.) Ives had first written a fugue with these subjects for Horatio Parker in 1897(?). He recomposed it (1898?) as part of the first movement of the *First String Quartet*, subtitled "A Revival Meeting."

Here, however, there is no necessity for tracing the sources of all of Ives' tunes and their original dates of composition before their incorporation into the *Fourth Symphony*. John Kirkpatrick's Preface to *The Fourth Symphony* covered this quite adequately.[16] Here we are more interested in determining the technical devices that

Ives uses by which consciousness is represented, and to determine the controls with which he selected his materials.

Consciousness has two parts: first, the association, and second, the flow. The association is a private activity that has as its essence the simple fact that people endure. This qualitative process of enduring is what identifies real or lived time from the artificial quantitative time of the mathematician.[17] It is an awareness of what goes on in ourselves. Memory is its basis, yet the quality is that of being sustained, of being able to pass from one level of consciousness to another. The second part, the flow, deals with the fact that the mind can focus on any one thing but momentarily, for one thing suggests another through the association of common qualities or mental links between totally separate ideas that at some past time were linked in some way in the private conscious or experience.

The flow is an important part of free-association. Such patterns of association, formed on the subconscious level, appear in the second movement of the *Fourth Symphony* with its connected web of more than fifteen tunes quoted, including "Columbia, the Gem of the Ocean," "Marching through Georgia," "Turkey in the Straw," "Camptown Races," "Throw out the Lifeline," "Yankee Doodle," and "Jesus, Lover of my Soul." Yet it would be sheerly a flight of imagination to attempt to outline the reasons why the thought of one tune brought on another. At times the rapid succession of tunes or the superimposition of one tune on another shows the interrelation or association of ideas, but the chief function of these multiple views is to express the flow, or movement. At the same time, a case can be made for the similarity of the intervalic structure of the quoted tunes in the last movement of the *Fourth Symphony*. (*Martyn* at 24 joins *Bethany* which begins the movement. *Missionary Chant* enters at 36, and an interchange of tunes, phrases and rhythms develops. *Martyn, Dorrnance, Missionary Chant, Proprior Deo, St. Hilda,* the *Westminster Chimes* and *As Freshmen First We Came to Yale* surround a quodlibet of Bethany at 64.)

According to Ives' notes written on the back of some old music manuscripts, the *Fourth Violin Sonata,* called "Children's Day at the Camp Meeting" is another psychical autobiography. Ives used some of its parts and suggested themes in organ and other earlier pieces. Ives says that "The subject matter is a kind of reflection, remembrance, expression, etc. of the children's services at the out-door

Summer camp meetings held around Danbury and in many of the farm towns in Connecticut, in the 70's, 80's, and 90's.

At the summer meetings, there was usually only one Children's Day, and according to Ives, an actual happening at one of these services suggested the first movement of the *Fourth Violin Sonata*.[18] The children sometimes would get excited and actually march to the more militant hymns. One day Lowell Mason's "Work for the Night is Coming" got the boys going. Naturally the loudest singers and also those with the best voices would sing most of the wrong notes, and the boys got almost as far off from Lowell Mason as they did from the organ.

The Largo following the first part intones "Yes, Jesus Loves Me," with all its connotations of Sunday school while the last movement asks plaintively "Shall We Gather at the River?" And when the listener must supply the missing phrase "That flows by the Throne of God" we have a suspension of mental content, (see Ex. 12, 13) a favorite device of stream-of-consciousness technique.[19]

EXAMPLE 12. Ives. *Fourth Violin Sonata.* "Children's Day at Camp Meeting," Movement II., p. 8. measure 1. Copyright by Associated Music Publishers. Used by permission. This exam-

ple illustrates the suspension of mental content. Ives quotes the first part of the old hymn "Yes, Jesus Loves Me," leaving the listener to supply (mentally) the answering phrase "the Bible tells me so."

("At The River" Lowry)

EXAMPLE 13. Ives. *Fourth Violin Sonata.* "Children's Day at Camp Meeting". Movement III, p. 19, measures 8–14. Copyright by permission. Ives never quotes the last phrase of "Shall We Gather at the River?" correctly. Here, he alters the phrase "that flows by the throne of God." At the conclusion of the movement, he simply leaves it out.

What Ives has done for his listener by making him supply the missing phrase is to force him into a re-creative function. Thus the flux of mental life centers on the privacy of the listener, and consciousness remains an enigma. This method of suspending sense impressions and ideas in the memory not only gives a private quality to the passage, but reinforces the memory, for it is a well-known psychological fact that man remembers best a task (or passage) that is interrupted or incomplete.

Aside from free association of tunes and memories, Ives uses certain mechanical controls to represent the movement of consciousness in music. These devices often signal the listener and the performer of certain changes or shifts in psychic time. They can be compared to Virginia Woolf's reliance on punctuation,

William Faulkner's use of italics in *The Sound and The Fury,* and John Dos Passos' "Newsreel" sections in his trilogy *U.S.A.*

Ives' use of nonmetrical melody interwoven in relatively free temporal relationships is an example of a stream-of-consciousness device. By omitting the basic "punctuation" of music—the meter signature and bar lines—Ives manages to exercise a kind of visual control. The "stream" itself is carefully controlled, as in *The Concord Sonata,* by the "fall" or "down" determined by the interplay of phrases. (See Ex. 14) Thus there is a periodic relationship by length,

III. "The Alcotts"

EXAMPLE 14. Ives. *Second Piano Sonata.* "The Alcotts", p. 53. Measures 1, 2, 3. Copyright by Associated Music Publishers. Used by permission.

accent, pause, emphasis, or silence. This lack of a meter signature and the scattered placement of bar lines also reinforces the stream of consciousness device of quoted tunes by forcing the performer to create his own phrase patterns according to his inner view and feeling for the musical content. Thus, each performance becomes unique and highly individual, and it is entirely possible that the same artist might play the same piece in any one of several completely different ways according to his whim. Since Ives indicates in many scores that the performer may add or omit notes or vary the dynamics, each performer is forced to serve not only as an interpreter but in a re-creative function, for he can see what he wishes in the music.

Yet there are problems in capturing the irrational and incoherent quality of private consciousness. Each individual keeps his own file of associations and memories which are confidential. Another consciousness often finds these same symbols an enigma, or incoherent. Listeners, moreover, expect that the composer have something to communicate and the composer, if he has something to say, has some sense of values he wants to communicate. Ives was serious about his composing; although his livelihood in no way depended upon his music, he often came in from work and immediately began composing, remaining at the piano until two or three in the morning. He also attempted to get his works performed, until having failed in his attempts so often, he gave up on public recognition. No one can doubt his seriousness. Nor can anyone doubt his sense of values; his writings, in particular, *Essays Before a Sonata,* display a well-thought out philosophy. If, as I maintain, Ives was deliberately attempting to present consciousness, he had to do two things: (1) represent the texture of consciousness, and (2) communicate some kind of meaning from it all. Since, for the most part, Ives did not write nonsense music, he carefully dropped clues to unravel his scheme throughout his work. Within his work, the basic principles of psychological free association are his guide, and his musical quotes are psychologically coherent and revealing, although they are at first puzzling to the casual listener. The point is that the listener must attempt to place himself within the mental framework of the composer's mind. Because Ives knows this and relies on the principle of association, he often goes out of his way to plunge the reader into his thought-stream. For example, he wrote the entire book *Essays Before a Sonata* to accompany *The Concord*

Sonata. His very generous use of familiar popular tunes also signals the perceptive listener of his special method. In addition, he often wrote remarkably clear instructions indicating exactly what each musical part meant to him. In the Foreword to *The Unanswered Question,* for example he states that

> . . . The strings play *ppp* throughout with no change in tempo. They are to represent "The Silences of the Druids—Who Know, See and Hear Nothing." The trumpet intones "The Perennial Question of Existence," and states it in the same tone of voice each time. But the hunt for "The Invisible Answer" undertaken by the flutes and other human beings, becomes gradually more active, faster and louder through an animando to a confuoco. This part need not be played in the exact time position indicated. It is played in somewhat of an impromptu way; if there be no conductor, one of the flute players may direct their playing. "The Fighting Answerers", as the time goes on, and after a "secret conference" seem to realize a futility, and begin to mock "The Question"—the strife is over for the moment. After they disappear, "The Question" is asked for the last time, and "The Silences" are heard beyond in "Undisturbed Solitude." . . . .[20]

In the *String Quartet No. 2* (1907-1913) Ives indicated the programmatic content of the quartet with this note: "String Quartet for four men who converse, discuss, argue (politics), fight, shake hands, shut up, then walk up the mountain side to view the firmament." The argument may have been over the Civil War, for in the first movement a strain from *Dixie* is announced, and in the second movement *Columbia the Gem of the Ocean* is followed by *Marching through Georgia.* In the third movement snippets out of Brahms' *Second Symphony* and Beethoven's *Ninth* are followed by *Nearer My God to Thee.* The quartet, a modern quodlibet, is in three movements: Discussions (andante moderato), Arguments (allegro con spirito), and The Call of the Mountains (adagio). The programmatic titles of the three movements are Ives' means of indicating the associations of his quoted tunes.

Another aspect of this is a series of remarks, written on the manuscript, addressed to Rollo, the second violin. Rollo is probably taken from a series of books for properly brought up and well-mannered New England boys, for he is conservative, genteel, and timid. One of his pretty little tunes is labelled "Andante Emasculata." His other musical phrases are pretty, traditional, and polite, for Rollo, to Ives, symbolizes narrow-minded, conservative tradition.

The dissonant arguments of the other players often break in on Rollo's timid musings, and he finally falls silent (bars 58–79) except for an outraged "tut-tut"! Poor feminine Rollo represented the side of music that embarrassed Ives. As a boy Ives was partially ashamed of music, which he, in some ways regarded as a "sissy-art." His own reaction against the weakness of musical art led him into a direct confrontation with Rollo, who also represented the authority-figure.

That the authority-figure was feminine was characteristic of "culture" in the latter part of the nineteenth century. Proper, well-brought-up-young-ladies "from good families" played sentimental music in the parlor on Sunday after church. This was the "serious" music of the genteel culture that Ives revolted against, and throughout his life he used feminine terms such as "ladybird," "sissy," and "old ladies" to refer to things in music that he disliked. Ives' sarcastic jibing ("Too hard to play—so it just can't be good music, Rollo.") expresses his resentment against the prevailing feminine music culture of the times. "Cut it out, Rollo!" he writes on his manuscript. "Beat time, Rollo!" he admonishes. "Join in again, Professor, all in the key of C. You can do that nice and pretty." Yet all the while that he attempts through such remarks to tell himself that music (and Rollo) doesn't matter, the resentment and cynicism of his contempt belie his true feelings. Raging against Rollo expressed the suffering he must have felt when a celebrated violinist came to play his music and made fun of it. The violinist, it seems, did not even get through the first page of the *First Violin Sonata*. The rhythms and notes perplexed him and he told Ives that "This cannot be played. . . . This is awful. . . . It is not music, it makes no sense." Finally he left, after remarking that "When you get awfully indigestible food in your stomach that distresses you, you can get rid of it. But I cannot get those horrible sounds out of my ears with a dose of castor oil." Apparently depressed, Ives felt for a while that there was something wrong with himself or he wouldn't write music that nobody liked. "ARE MY EARS ON WRONG?" he wondered.[21]

The marginal persiflage on *String Quartet No. 2* and the baiting of Rollo are revealing psychologically, but peripheral to the point. The point is simply the presentation of free discussion, and Ives, through his notes and marginalia on the score, wants to make it clear that this is what his quartet is "about."

Besides the basic method of free association, Ives employed other devices to achieve the tone and texture of consciousness. These are, musically speaking, analogous to the rhetorical means used by stream-of-consciousness authors. Although practically any passage of writing or music will contain these "rhetorical devices," it is over-use of these means, the piling-up of them that is a characteristic of stream-of-consciousness works. These devices include hyperbaton (the violation of the usual order of words, or in the case of music, the placing of the second phrase of the tune ahead of the first); anaphora (the repetition of a word or musical idea at the beginning of clauses or phrases); ellipsis (the omission of one or more words, or parts of a tune phrase, obviously understood, necessary to make the expression complete), and anacoluthon (the abandonment in the midst of a sentence of one type of construction in favor of one grammatically or musically different.) The use of these constructions, in English, is a characteristic of stream-of-consciousness fiction.[22] Hyperbaton and ellipsis are illustrated by the melodically altered fragments from "The Battle Hymn of the Republic" quoted in "Lincoln the Great Commoner." Examples of anacoluthon abound in the Second Piano Sonata. (See Ex. 15) William Faulkner's *As I Lay Dying* and *The Sound and the Fury,* and James Joyce's *Ulysses* are good literary examples that constantly use these means.

Anaphora, the repetition of a word or musical idea at the beginning of clauses or phrases is purposely illustrated by *The Unanswered Question.* The trumpet intones "the question" with the same tone and (all but one) of the same notes each time throughout the piece, mocked by the flutes at the last.

Still another device Ives and other stream-of-consciousness creators resorted to is the use of symbols. When music draws heavily upon existing material, as in the quotations of Ives, such music possesses an internal symbolism. Ives, for example, often resuscitated past musical expressions such as church hymns, vaudeville tunes, sentimental parlor songs of the early nineteenth century and band tunes. This type of borrowing emphasized the symbolism of musical emotions by what was presented to hearing, and the use of quoted material in this way was a ready-made symbol of the specific musical feelings it embodied. Symbolism in music based on prior association simply meant that a tune that has acquired meaning in another way (such as Dixie) comes to represent some-

thing, be it a happening, emotion, or abstract conception, when
it is imported into a musical composition.

EXAMPLE 15. Ives. Second Piano Sonata, "Concord," "Hawthorne",
           p. 41. Measures 1, 2, 3. Copyright by Associated Music Pub-
           lishers. Used by permission. Anacoluthon, or the abandon-
           ment of one type of construction for one musically different
           is illustrated by this example from the third movement of
           the *Concord Sonata*. Anacoluthon is frequently found in all
           the movements of *The Concord Sonata*.

This musical material brought its meaning with it sheerly by
the fact of association. Quoted tunes, of course, assumed a knowledge on the part of the listener for the particular connection with
the past. Ives was concerned with the relation of symbolism to
reality. He asked himself if all inspirational images, states, conditions, or whatever they may be called had for a dominant part,
if not for a source, some actual experience in life or of the social

relation. Ives thought it would be a relief if such images or symbols did not have a source in actual reality, but "it seems difficult to suppose that even subconscious images can be separated from some human experience; there must be something behind subconsciousness to produce consciousness, and so on." [23]

Naturally, symbols are often not defined since symbols are by nature indefinable. The associations and the ideas come later in the listener's mind after hearing the symbol (quoted tune). Symbolism in music as a basic technique is not new. Borrowed tunes, an essence of musical symbolism, can be found in works from previous centuries. From our earliest recorded musical history both sacred and secular tunes were quoted by other composers. "Borrowing" itself is no innovation; some early English songs seem to be imitations of liturgical music; for instance, the songs attributed to St. Godric who died in 1170.[24] Even in that century borrowing was not a new procedure. Motets, clausula, parody masses and quodlibets were all old forms often incorporating some older dance or song tune in the composition.

Yet most of these composers who have borrowed tunes have not been concerned with the associations the listener might have with the tune. For example, when Beethoven uses the trite little waltz by Diabelli as the basis for his *Thirty-three Variations in C Major, Op. 120,* he is borrowing Diabelli's intervallic relations and using the tune as thematic material. He is not particularly concerned with the memories a listener might have upon hearing the waltz-tune. Similarly, Brahms famous *Variations on a Theme by Haydn* for two pianos has as its theme the *Choral: St. Antoni.* Yet the *Choral* suggests no obvious extra musical images. Unlike Ives, most of the composers who have borrowed tunes have not been concerned with the associations the listener might have with the tune, but are more concerned with intervallic relations and the tune as thematic material. Ives as a stream of consciousness artist, on the other hand, uses familiar tunes to communicate something outside of a musical pattern. He emphasizes borrowed tunes because of their nonmusical meaning.

Ives uses montage, a technique whose function is presenting either more than one object or more than one tune simultaneously to demonstrate that our consciousness is more often than not a strange conglomeration of interlocking ideas. The second movement of the *Fourth Symphony* is a good example of an interlocking of rhythmic ideas on many different levels. Here a kaleidoscope of interactions shows conflicting melodies and particles of musical ideas that often disintegrate before maturing. John Kirkpatrick writes:

> The comedy movement also starts with two great sighs in the bass. . . . A quieter part (#23)—a "take off here on polite salon music . . . pink teas in Vanity Fair social life"—leads to some of the Hawthorne ragtime (an irreverent version of the "human-faith-melody" is in the left hand of the solo piano, 3 before 27 and 3 before #30—also the Beethoven theme fragmented in the trumpets between #31 and #32 while the trombones blare out *Beulah Land,* the cornets sing the "Down in the cornfield" phrase from Foster's *Massa's in de Cold Ground,* and the solo piano bangs out *In the Sweet By and By.*) . . .[25]

Music exists independently on different planes in this movement, and also in the work *Central Park in the Dark. The New River,* for chorus and orchestra, also juxtaposes musical ideas without any transitions. The important thing about this use of montage is that it not only shows an interrelation or association of ideas or the superimposition of image on image, but it shows composite views of one subject.

Ives himself once wrote that "an apparent confusion, if lived with long enough, may become orderly." [26] In fact, he believed that a clearer scoring might have lowered the thought. The thought was the thing, but what was the thought? For Ives the intellect was never a whole, but only a track to the over-values.[27] And his basic techniques for presenting all the levels of consciousness posed the same problems that authors of stream-of-consciousness fiction puzzled over.

In conclusion, then, the philosopher-psychologists, William James and Henri Bergson, developed the idea that consciousness contained basically two parts: first, the association (durée) and second, the flow, or stream. They achieved the difficult job of depicting this consciousness through utilizing the psychological principles of free association. That is, one memory (tune), always brings up another, through a previous emotional association, thereby giving the listener a system to follow. Additional devices borrowed from literary techniques conveyed the sense of discontinuity of the consciousness. Ives used certain mechanical devices to represent the texture of consciousness, and he communicated his meaning by carefully dropped clues—program notes and the like. From many points of view Ives examined the complexity of time and memory until the past emerged as part of the living present.

4

LOOKING BACKWARD: REALISM REVISITED

TRANSCENDENTALISM WAS MOTHER TO A number of movements with profound effect on American culture. Realism was one offspring of Transcendentalism.[1] Emerson embraced the common, the familiar, and the low because he saw in them the link to a higher world. "Every natural fact is a symbol of some spiritual fact," wrote Emerson.[2] He recommended the study of nature as one of the best ways to gain knowledge of the Absolute or Over-Soul, the essence that pervaded all things. Thus the practical and spiritual world were united and the groundwork laid for America's belief in science and progress as a means to utopia. Indeed, the Emersonian vocabulary helps to explain the connection between realism and utopian visions. It also explains the combinations of different traits, survivals of the past, mannerisms, and anticipations of the future that cause so much confusion in defining "realism."

Realism, obviously, is a pluralistic term. There are many realisms, and every past work of art or literature has had its realistic elements. "Heroes and villains, if they were to command belief," writes George J. Becker, "had to have some saving touch of nature." [3] Realistic details thus do not constitute realism, for realism is more than "the art of depicting nature as it is seen by toads." [4] As in literature, determining what constitutes realism in music is a messy affair. But although the design is complex, there is a "figure in the carpet." This figure seems to have four points: first, a subject matter chosen from the interests and ideals of the common people; second, a technique exploring the subjective, subconscious side of man; third, exactness and universality of representation; and fourth, a fundamental moral orientation.

Charles Ives, like the literary realists, chose his subject matter from a middle ground. He rejected the sights of the sewers as well as the "pretty little sugarplums" of the ideal. His concern was with the sights and sounds of the common life, with the average experience, with what Alfred Kazin calls "the whole cluster of experiences which make up the native culture." [5] Ives' realism in subject matter took two forms, an attempt to visually reproduce a scene through musical notation, and programmatic titles and essays designed to show that he is basing his music on middle-class concerns.

Ives' attempt to make music concrete, apart from the transitory effects of sound is a relation not only to the Transcendental idea (borrowed from the Greeks) of "music of the spheres," but also to the realists' extension of the subject matter previously available. In "Some Quarter-Tone Impressions" Ives implies that the subject matter of music is more than sound. He remarks that the extension of medium, of physical material, the processes of which are continuously occurring in some department of art, does not necessarily imply new material, for the selection and use of different vibration numbers in some orderly plan is not new in the history of music. Many peoples and countries, ancient and modern, use smaller tone divisions than Western man. Ives thinks that more and more premises of truth are coming before man, "though to hold that music is built on unmovable, definitely known laws of tone which rule so as to limit music in all of its manifestations is better—but not much—than brushing everything aside except ecstatic ebullitions and a cigarette." [6]

This is the same idea that Ives plays with in the *Essays Before a Sonata* when he remarks that "Music may be yet unborn. Perhaps no music has ever been written or heard." [7] Much earlier in his life his father had admonished him not to pay attention to the off-key bellowings of old John the stonemason, or he would miss the music. "Look into his face and hear the music of the ages. Don't pay too much attention to the sounds. If you do, you may miss the music." [8] This idea that music could be viewed subconsciously as well as heard, greatly impressed Ives, who would later write, "that music must be heard is not essential—what it sounds like may not be what it is. Perhaps the day is coming when music-believers will learn that silence is a solvent . . . that gives us leave to be universal rather than personal." [9] In a more explosive frame of mind he writes, "My God! What has sound got to do with music!" [10]

If music is a subconscious vision of infinity having little to do with sound, then the door to the subjective is wide open, and Ives can offer his temperamental reactions to life as if they were the result of a most careful weighing-up of the whole universe. In this way, parts of his music that bewilder the ear reach out (at least to Ives) into a world which has its own meaning. Thus the mind, which many psychologists seem to think sees in pictures, combines visual notation with the idea of sound. For example, the camp meetings that Ives attended as a boy seemed to him a marvelous personal and social experience to be graphically depicted. Since several hundred people sing various versions of the correct pitch, Ives tries realistically to reproduce what actually goes on by surrounding a melody with a wide band of tones. Thus melodies are composed of groups of cluster-chords to reproduce the effects of mass singing. The *Third* and *Fourth Symphonies* contain examples of. this, yet the effect heard by the listener is not the same as the effect of a camp-meeting. Ives with his keen ear must have known this. So the attempt is either to reproduce the emotional effect or a combination visual-sound effect. The bases of notation are both visual and auditory equivalences that are more than arbitrary, as Edward Lippman has shown, for intersensory connections are involved in the representation of pitch along a visual dimension, and auditory duration is projected at least partly in terms of visually perceived length. [11] "Some nice people object to putting attempted pictures of American authors and their literature in a thing called a sonata," Ives writes, "but I don't apologize for it or explain it. . . ." [12] Again, he has written on the back of an organ postlude, *Thanksgiving and Forefathers Day* that "Our forefathers were stronger men than can be represented by triads only—these are too easy sounding."

That this view of Ives' music mixes literary or musical realism with philosophical realism goes without saying. Philosophical realism, of course, is compatible with an immense variety of doctrines. Briefly, philosophical realism is defined as "the theory of the reality of abstract or general terms, or universals which are held to have an equal and sometimes a superior reality to actual physical partic-

ulars. . . . Realism (is) as real as, if not more real than, the realm
of existence, or actuality." [13] Ives' realism, in fact, concludes that
the subjective experience is the only objective experience.[14] This
view identifies impressionism and states of mind with realism and
in doing so turns the nineteenth century meaning of realism up-
sidedown, replacing it with an individual, atomistic, subjective
realism in the sense of Proust and Bergson. Ives as a realist thus
commits himself to relativity and complexity. He writes:

> Some say "Why choose local authors for a reason for music?—people
> will say you are provincial." . . . I say "O Hell!" to this label-monger!
> If a man is born in a sewer, he smells it and of it—(but he may
> be nearer a spiritual fragrance than the mayor:) God lives somewhere
> in the Heavens—but ain't he universal? Emerson lives in Mas-
> sachusetts—and he's as universal as any writer. . . .[15]

The second form that Ives' realism in subject matter takes is his
sympathy with the common people. This sympathy manifests
through his choice of song texts, and choice of quoted tunes considered aside from their musical content. When his subjects are people,
they are the middle-class-backbone-of-the-country variety like
"Aunt Sarah who scrubbed her life away for her brother's ten
orphans." [16] "The Greatest Man" is a song about a little boy's
father; "Lincoln" is the "Great Commoner"; "Charlie Rutlage"
is a cowboy; "Tom Sails Away" is the song of the common soldier.
Yet all of Ives' character subjects bear a trade-mark—they are
imaginatively representative of the common experience, the statistical norm.

When his subject is the outdoor milieu, the topography is New
England America: *Three Places in New England* featuring the Boston
Common, Putnam's Camp, and the River Housatonic at Stock-
bridge; *The Concord Sonata* depicting Concord, Massachusetts;
Orchestra Set No. 2 with four movements, "An Elegy to Our Fore-
fathers," "The Rockstrewn Hills Join in the People's Outdoor Meet-
ing," and "From Hanover Square North at the End of a Tragic
Day" and "Central Park in the Dark."

The historical element of Ives' choice of subject matter involves
local color and conditions and manners particularly common to
the American experience. Ives set himself a severe standard for
the depiction of contemporary life with minute precision. Ives' way
out is to commemorate holidays through music, an act which

besides dealing with customs, takes on frequently a philological aspect. "An Election," "Anti-Abolitionist Riots," "Decoration Day," "Fourth of July," "Halloween," "Holidays," and "New England Holidays—i. Washington's Birthday, ii. Decoration Day, iii. Fourth of July, iv. Thanksgiving and/or Forefathers' Day"—are a few sets that show his preoccupation with conditions and manners indigenous to America. As an historian of American holidays, Ives was a master of impressionistic effect, an oblique crusader for democracy, a psychologist of childhood, and on occasion, an unsurpassed humorist.

All of the realists agreed with Emerson's dictum not to seek outside the self.[17] Their views that the subconscious was an essential part of the "reality" of man were later developed by Freud's work, but years before Freud's speculations, human motives and thoughts were as graphically depicted as other areas of human activity. Confusion exists concerning this exploration of what Dostoevsky termed "the underground man," since many claim, along with George Becker that "the basic ideal of the movement was and is absolute objectivity."[18] Yet as Harold H. Kolb points out, this is simply not the case.[19] The realists do not achieve or even attempt to achieve absolute objectivity, though they may strive for the illusion of objectivity.

The technique that Ives uses to explore the subjective is the same technique that many authors of realistic fiction used in their attempts to unravel the complexities and multiplicities of experience. For the realists, the truth is complex, and life is a complicated and ambiguous affair. The best way to express this theme was to create a work of interwoven, entangled physical density. This represented the complexity of experience. At the same time the work should contain multiple points of view to express the simultaneous existence of different levels of reality.

The complexity in Ives generally consists of several elements: tediousness (a repetition of notes that come from nowhere and go nowhere), mediocrity (a common-place passage of no particular import), sociological features (such as a quoted tune), universality (a passage impossible for a certain instrument to play), a correspondence with internal reality (musical passages with no transitions.) (See Ex. 16, 17, 18)

All this may go on in one instrumental voice, or in several. If it goes on at the same time in several instruments, such as in the second movement of the *Fourth Symphony,* multiplicity of experience represents reality in all its forms. The extreme difficulty in

EXAMPLE 16. Ives. "Cradle Song." Copyright 1933 Merion Music. Used by permission of the publisher. Example of tediousness, phrases that go nowhere. "Cradle Song" from *114 Songs* has a tonally-static melody that cadences on G# for each phrase.

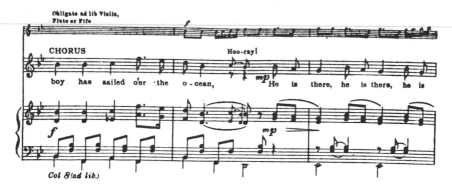

EXAMPLE 17. Ives. "He Is There!" *114 Songs* (private printing, C. E. Ives). Examples of sociological feature, such as a quoted tune.

"He is There!" contains phrases from "O Columbia The Gem of the Ocean!"

Majority

EXAMPLE 18. Ives. "The Majority." P. 1, second, third and fourth systems. Copyright 1933, Merion Music, Inc. Used by permission of the publisher. An example of universality of expression, passages impossible to play with regular means.

such a technique lies in arousing the emotional tone which a tremendous weight of details evokes on the part of those embroiled in them. Since more than one idea at a time was present, logical transitions fell by the wayside, and anyhow, the realists realized that the subconscious was in continuous flux and change, an idea that negated developmental transitions. The technique then, was patch-work—collections of fragments, motifs, genre scenes, scraps, and pieces.

Symphony No. 3, in the first movement illustrates overlapping quotations in both the horn and second violin parts from the hymn *Azmon.* (See Ex. 19) Later the *Azmon* hymn is in canon. Also, the

EXAMPLE 19. Ives. *Symphony No. 3,* p. 3. At 2. Measures 1-4. Copyright by Associated Music Publishers. Used by permission.

second violin melody changes to different levels. Hymns and the organ pieces Ives played in the Central Presbyterian Church provided the themes for this symphony. *Children's Day Parade,* for string quartet and organ formed the middle movement. Polytonality also enters the picture. The last two measures of the third movement are polytonal, with B minor–G sharp minor against B flat major and F major.

The complexity and multiplicity in Ives' work is more than matched by his ambiguous endings, another characteristic of realists. The realistic preference of novelists, as seen in the endings of the novels of the mid-1880's, revels in the ambiguous and the unresolved.[20] *The Bostonians* by Henry James, for example ends inconclusively.

"Ah, now I am glad," said Verena when they reached the street. But though she was glad, Basil presently saw that . . . . she was in tears. It is to be feared that with the union, so far from brilliant, into which she was about to enter, these were not the last she was destined to shed.[21]

In *The American*, Christopher Newman loses the woman he loves and in renouncing revenge, is left with neither innocence nor experience. As Mrs. Tristram remarks at the end, "My impression would be that since, as you say, they defied you, it was because they believed that after all, you would never really come to the point. . . ."[22] William Dean Howells' novels also just stop, rather than conclude, and seldom is anything resolved. Mark Twain's works are also opposed to neatly contrived resolutions and sentimental endings.

The same ambiguity in endings found in realistic literature muffles the endings of many of Ives' pieces. The first movement of the *Concord Sonata*, for example, simply disintegrates: the dynamic level falls to *pp, ppp, pppp*, the tempo retards, the last two measures are marked with fermatas to further hold back the movement, while

*) To be heard as a kind of an overtone

EXAMPLE 20. Ives. *The Second Piano Sonata*, "Concord," p. 20. Final 7 measures. Copyright by Associated Music Publishers. Used by permission. The ending disintegrates, as this example shows.

a minor third (C sharp to E natural) is heard as a kind of overtone interrupted at the very last by the bass sounding the motive A to F natural, forte. (See Ex. 20)

Similarly, the endings of many of his other pieces are incomplete. "Lincoln the Great Commoner" is an even more curious example since the ending is a quoted fragment from "The Star Spangled Banner." This same example shows the use of unresolved dissonance, a C major triad plus A minor plus the whole tones F#, G#, A#, a polychordal structure.[23] The last part of the phrase "Shall we gather at the river" which is quoted in "Children's Day at the Camp Meeting" is also left incomplete at the end. (See Ex. 21, 22) Probability and human nature often leave problems unsolved, so Ives' endings are often confessions of the irresolvable complexities of life.

The exactness and universality of representation of Ives' realism assumes the form of quoted tunes, for the great constructive element in art is the interaction of the artist with the continuity of tradition. Not surprisingly, Ives' practice of musical quotation spans his whole work. Originality, independent of invention, seizes the latent possibilities of familiar things, and familiar things in Ives' case are musical experiences of all kinds, times, and cultures. His imagery grows out of the essential character of the quoted tune, but the imagery carries with it as a corollary a mass of memories. This richness of assimilation of what tradition furnishes gives to the music a body, a fullness. The vitality of traditional tunes in a sense lessens the importance of the individual composer and leans toward omniscient narration. Ives' emphasis on substance rather than manner furnishes the evidence: "In a word, when he [the composer] becomes conscious that his style is his personal own, that it has monopolized a geographical part of the world's sensibilities—then it may be that the value of his substance is not growing, that it even may have started on its way backwards."[24] Ives goes on to say that the composer should be open to all the over-values and "lessons of the infinite that humanity has received and thrown to man".[25]

Many of Ives' quoted tunes assume epic significance. (See Ex. 23) The motif of Beethoven's *Fifth Symphony,* the so-called "fate" motive was, for Ives, so great a theme that he considered it universal in nature with implications that should continue to grow and to be incorporated into new music.[26]

EXAMPLE 21. Ives. "At the River." Copyright 1933, Merion Music, Inc.
Used by permission of the publisher. Final 6 measures.

Ives is a vernacular virtuoso who commands a wide range
of imagery. He makes the listener "look with his ears" at common

things by re-creating them so they take on the coloration of his
point of view. Colloquial American speech culminates in key moments in "Charlie Rutlage" and "Nov. 2, 1920." "Soliloquy," on

EXAMPLE 22. Ives. Fourth Violin Sonata. "Children's Day at the Camp-
meeting." P. 2, measures 7–14. Copyright by Associated
Music Publishers. Used by permission.

EXAMPLE 23. Ives. *Second Piano Sonata,* First Movement (p. 2) The "fate"
motive is in accented half notes. (Beethoven's *Symphony No.*
5). Copyright by Associated Music Pub., used by permission.

the other hand, would be fiendishly hard to sing in spite of the fact that Ives describes it (innocuously) as "an attempt at a take-off of the Yankee drawl. . . . a study in sevenths and other things." [27]

   Yet song-texts more often than not use informal speech style. (See Ex. 24, 25) For instance, Ives often uses notation without a meter and sometimes without a definite pitch level, or only a suggested level, as in "Grantchester". He may also insert a yell or other nonmusical cry in the score, as in "He is There!"

December

EXAMPLE 24. Ives. "December." Copyright 1933, Merion Music. Used by permission of the publisher. Song illustrates informal speech style.

Soliloquy
or a Study in 7ths and Other Things

EXAMPLE 25. Ives. "Soliloquy". Copyright 1933, Merion Music. Used by permission of the publisher. Song illustrates informal speech style.

   Ives' personal use of the vernacular runs all through his homey *Essays Before a Sonata,* and he did not seem averse to using the all-American God-damn on occasion. Once during the performance of Carl Ruggles' "Men and Mountains" Ives stood up and shouted at a heckler: "Stop being such a God-damned sissy! Why can't you stand up before fine strong music like this and use your ears like a man!" [28] The remark was calculated, no doubt, to put both the heckler and the music into proper perspective.

Perceptive readers have long been aware of the fundamental moral orientation of American realism. [29] The realists explore the relations between man and society in many ways, yet their works demonstrate ethical concerns. The ethical concerns of the realists are different from those of the naturalists, who stressed the fatalistic mechanistic aspects of the universe, the materialism of man, and the commonplace and coarser forms of life. Since realism came to the United States much later than it had to the European Continent, American realism missed much of what is called naturalist determinism. The rigorous causality of naturalism with man as the hapless victim did not quite fit the fluid society of America. Moreover, the American sense of mission, optimism, and Protestant millennialism would not accept the pessimism inherent in naturalism.

Like his counterparts in the literary world, Ives came to conventional conclusions about morality. He sought intrinsic values, standard virtues like honesty, justice, love, and compassion. This affirmation of basic human values that runs all through the *Essays* had earlier permeated Transcendentalism, and the deep religiosity of Ives' heart can be heard beating in the many hymn tunes quoted in his musical compositions. For Ives, the fabric of life weaves itself whole, so he develops his moral themes with his secular tunes, often weaving them together. The *First Piano Sonata*, for example, uses fragments of "How Dry I Am," "Bringing in the Sheaves," and "I Hear Thy Welcome Voice" in ragtime rhythm. The second movement of the *Fourth Symphony* is, of course, the greatest compendium of sacred-secular tunes.

From the number of gospel hymns quoted, Ives apparently thought that the ethical content of music was so essential that it demanded a place as an integral part of his realism. Although there is probably no way to prove this, Ives' emphasis on religious tunes seems to indicate the morality of his realism, and is not, as is sometimes thought, simply another manifestation of his musical contrariness. Ives' ability to adopt the musical point of view of the child might also be a means of conveying morality.

This realistic technique used by Ives is the pose of innocence, the point of view of the naive narrator. As an unsophisticated innocent, Ives can be unconventional and humorous, or in a rare mood, very simple, as in "The Greatest Man" which is narrated by a little boy:

> My teacher said us boys should write about some great man, so I thought last night n' thought about heroes and men that had done great things, n' then I got to thinkin' 'bout my pa; he ain't a hero 'r anything—but pshaw! Say!—He can ride the wildest hoss 'n find minners near the moss down by the creek; 'n he can swim 'n fish. . . .[30]

For once the piano accompaniment trots right along with the voice which is to be sung "In a half boasting and half wistful way, not too fast or too evenly."

The composer's pose of naivete (and pretend ignorance) prevents him from making evaluations of the blatant noises and crude vulgarity of some music; he is free just to write it down. So the trite marching tune of "The Circus Band" hiccups in literal imitation, with notes written in to deliberately sound like mistakes (which all town amateur bands enthusiastically, and often unconsciously, played). "The Circus Band" and another circus piece, "The Side Show" involve the kind of literal imitation that exemplifies the realists' movement away from editorializing.

"Innocence" as a musical guise had its counterpart in literature. Such books as Alcott's *Little Women* and *Little Men,* Aldrich's *Story of a Bad Boy,* Howell's *A Boy's Town* and *Years of My Youth* were only part of the fiction idealizing childhood and the theme of innocence. "Innocence," best dramatized in terms of childhood, was one means of reliving the past that sometimes had archetypal significance and expressed subconscious desires. Mark Twain, for example, writing largely under the influence of unconscious impulses, recounted in his first book *Innocents Abroad* the way the sensitive, innocent individual was trapped by history. His other travel narratives, and especially *Roughing It,* involved the same theme. The intent and form of such sensibilities was developed in Henry James' novels. *A Small Boy and Others* retained the same sort of innocence, a kind of openness to impressions that earlier symbolized the American Adam, Christopher Newman in *The American.*

Such openness was often nondiscriminating; trivia-and-truth entered side by side. E. E. Cummings in *Six Non-Lectures* wrote that "In the course of my six half-hours of egocentricity I shall (among other deeds) discuss the difference between fact and truth, I shall describe professor Royce and the necktie crisis, I shall name professor Charles Eliot Norton's coachman, and I shall define sleep. If you ask "but why include trivialities?" my answer will be: what are they?" [31] To the innocent, whose Eden still maintained visiting-hours, endless details and semi-identical superficialities were as important as esoteric and recondite doctrine. Mixing the important and the nonimportant located man out of history altogether.

Ives focuses an innocent ear on romantic conventions, sentimentality and camp meetings, knowing full well that the listener's awareness depends on his mature understanding. He writes for children who are quite old. "Two Little Flowers" is sly sentiment mixed with irony (The marigold is radiant, the rose passing fair); "Childrens' Day at Camp Meeting" swings into a jazzy setting of a hymn and ends with a disturbed and incomplete question, "Shall we gather at the river?"; and the comedy of complexity in the second movement of the *Fourth Symphony* with its potpourri of misquoted tunes blares out Fourth-of-July celebrations. The list is endless, and the satire of the "innocent ear" is endlessly effective and a product of the realistic point of view.

The use of the "innocent ear" provides the disproportion and incongruity on which irony depends. The ironic view, a split view, works on many levels because it implies perception and sophistication on the part of the listener. Ives is both in on the joke and out of it. As he once wrote of the second song in a group of five street songs:

> This song (and the same may be said of others) is inserted for association's sake—on the ground that that will excuse anything; also, to help clear up a long disputed point, namely: which is worse, the music or the words? [32]

While the "innocent ear" of Ives and the literary realists indicated a kind of psychic retreat from actuality, it likewise showed through its irony that the mythical past was perpetually dissolving.

5

IVES, REVIVALISM, AND THE SOCIAL GOSPEL

THE POLITICAL CONFUSION AND CORRUP-
tion of the gilded age did not pass unnoticed. Earlier in the 1870's
clergymen such as Washington Gladden began to recognize the
unethical and unchristian elements in the exploitation of the wage
earner, and after 1880 this concern of the church with social matters
burgeoned. The concern with reforming society at large rather than
converting individuals was partially a result of Darwin's theory.
The firm fundamental beliefs of many were demolished by Darwin's
temporal relatedness, and many Christians were ready to accept
a compromise, "Christian evolution," which suggested that God
unfolded the Creation little by little through the years. This led
to new ideas of a Christian's duty in enforcing social justice so
that God's plan could be expedited.

But this "Social Gospel" preached by a few "liberal" Christians
failed to touch many. Those from rural backgrounds who felt
threatened by the alien city, and those city people who needed
a religion a plain man could understand, found solace in a more
fundamental religion and in revivals. Revivalism stressed two main
points: first was the importance of emotion in religion; second was
the significance of the individual. The salvation of the individual
was the chief goal of the revival.[1] Thus the revival allowed intuition
to triumph over rationality and innocence over experience. In this
way the fundamentalism of the past could psychically triumph
over the "new" and industrial present. The need to rebel was thus
partially a reaction against progress and not a forerunner of progress

itself. Ives, who exemplified this kind of rebellious reconstruction of the past, also thoroughly believed in the dogma of the social gospel—the "myth" of progress. His favorite hymn "Watchman, Tell Us of the Night" (Lowell Mason, 1831), which forms the core of the first movement of the *Fourth Symphony*, dramatizes the role of utopian progress, that escape from historic time.

> Watchman, tell us of the night
> What the signs of promise are:
> Traveler, o'er yon mountain's height,
> See that Glory-beaming star!
> Watchman, aught of joy or hope?
> Traveler, yes; it brings the day,
> Promised day of Israel.
> Dost thou see its beauteous ray?
>
> (Lowell Mason, 1831) [2]

That Ives may also have seen himself as the "watchman" is not an impossibility. His later breakdown was partially psychosomatic and may have been brought on by the frustration of his fantastic hopes by World War I. The war seemed to prove that the night was closing in, and the watchman a near-sighted idealist who had mistakenly called the threats of totalitarianism "signs of promise."

Religion in Ives' music and thought takes two forms. First, Ives reiterated the ideas and emotionalism characteristic of revivalism. Second, Ives adopted the more sophisticated beliefs in progress and utopia of the social gospellers, for concomitant with the rise of the social gospel were the great revivals of the 1870's and 1880's that were in essence, battles of the moderns versus the fundamentalists. Although hell was cooling off for the social gospellers, its flames still raged for the revivalists, for revivalism was *not* social gospel, but conservative. And while Ives' thought reflected the theory of the social gospellers, much of his music paralleled revival sermons in rhythm, programmatic content, and audience response to be evoked. From this cross fire and countercurrent emerged the unevenness of much of Ives' work, echoing the revival preachers of his youth.

The rise of the Social Gospel (social Christianity) helped generate the revivals, for revivals generally occur during a theological reorientation within the churches, a process connected with a general intellectual reorientation in society at large. An ecclesiastical

conflict associated with this reorientation helps stress the person-
alities of certain evangelicals dissatisfied with the prevailing order.
This dissatisfaction results from a social and spiritual cleavage both
within the churches and between the churches and the world. This
periodic reexamination and redefinition of the nation's social and
intellectual values results in a feeling on the part of those outside
the churches that Christianity might have a particular relevance
to their contemporary situation both individually and corporately.[3]

During the great revivals of Ives' youth[4] the country shifted
from an agrarian to an industrial economy, from rural to urban,
from anticolonial to imperialistic views, from a homogeneous to
a polygenetic people, and from a system of relative laissez-faire
to the first stages of national governmental social control. The influx
of immigrants brought into new focus the traditions of American
life. These changes registered most heavily on country-bred senti-
mentally insecure and uneducated individuals. Their insecurity
made them especially vulnerable to the revivalist preacher's "Come
forward and be saved" call.

Revivalism was conservative. The Social Gospel was liberal.
The chief difference between the revivalists and the social gospellers
was in their view of the best way to reform society. The revivalists
put their faith in reforming individuals while the social gospellers
put their faith in changing man's environment. The revivalists
wanted laws against drink, gambling, theater and dancing; the
social gospellers wanted laws to restrict the evil tendencies of mo-
nopolies, political machines, and fraudulent business practices.
Dwight L. Moody, a fundamentalist revival preacher whose greatest
influence was from 1873–1883 believed, for example, that society
could be reformed by the regeneration of individuals, and that
all political, social, and economic reform must be an appendage
of revivals.

Since revivals, according to these evangelicals, were the key
to reform, they had to attract the people. Revivalists, therefore,
began to apply commercial techniques, while at the same time
associating faith with a literal Bible and an orthodox theological
framework. Flamboyant crusades, incantations, rituals, and mass-
crowd-psychology jazzed up the religious experience. Such sensa-
tionalism often paralleled the circus atmosphere, and the deep
emotional fervor of the true believers contributed to the burlesque.

Ives reflected many of the ideas characteristic of revivalism. As a boy he had witnessed outdoor camp-meeting services in Redding where farmers, field hands, and townspeople from miles around would come on foot or in farm wagons.

> I remember how the great waves of sound used to come through the trees when things like *Beulah Land, Woodworth, Nearer My God to Thee, The Shining Shore, Nettleton, In the Sweet Bye-and-Bye* and the like were sung by thousands of "let-out" souls. The music notes and words on paper are about as much like what they were at those moments as the monogram on a man's necktie may be like his face. Father, who led the singing, sometimes with his cornet or his voice, sometimes with both voice and arms, and sometimes in the quieter hymns with a violin or French horn, would always encourage the people to sing their own way. Most of them knew the words and music (their version) by heart and sang it that way. If they threw the poet or composer around a bit, so much the better for the poetry and the music. There was power and exaltation in these great conclaves of sound from humanity.[5]

Ives, deeply impressed by this fervor, translated the emotional experience of the revival into his music. He did this in several ways: first, through direct imitation; second, through the creation of a psychological experience, and third, through form and structure.

Ives directly imitated the revival by quoting gospel hymns such as "Shall We Gather at the River?" and "Throw Out the Lifeline!" in his music. Revivals were loud, noisy affairs with hundreds of people singing different versions of the pitch. Ives used these same extremes of dynamics, often writing a dynamic marking of *FFFFF* or *ppppp*. Torrents of sound from his heavy scoring could indicate mass participation, and the continuous outpouring of sound was similar to the revival preacher's rhetoric, which partly depended upon his steady verbosity and blather for his hypnotic effect. The confusion and dissonance of camp-meetings became the florid stylistic tendency of much of Ives' music that reflected the revival, a gathering of many individuals, each expressing himself in his own way.

Ives, like the revival preachers, was in philosophy a conservative but in language, a revolutionary. His critics may have laughed, but Ives, ignoring their scoffing with admirable aplomb, brings back memories of the equally insurgent Billy Sunday who remarked, "They say I rub the fur the wrong way. *I* say, let the cats turn around!" [6] Stylistically, both Ives and the revivalists were way out front. Where some earlier religious evangelicals like Jonathan Edwards had used conventional literary language, the revivalists of the progressive era denounced sin and preached their "throw-a-nickel-in-the-plate-and-you'll-be-saved" doctrine in clear and common language. Gifted preachers attacked the devil, liquor, and prostitution (in approximately that order), and their language left no room for doubt or interpretation. Billy Sunday, baseball player and rigid reactionary, was famous for his plain talk and stinging rebukes. He once called a man who drank a "dirty, low-down, whisky-soaked, beer-guzzling, bull-necked, foul-mouthed hypocrite." [7] Sunday's effectiveness lay in his common speech and earthy slang as well as his virile denunciations. In his famous sermon "The Sins of Society", he injected pungent slang in astounding proportions:

> When the entertainment was at its height, Herodias shoved Salome out into the room to do her little stunt. He said to her: "Go like a twin-six!" She had anklets and bracelets on, but she didn't have clothes enough on her to flag a hand car. And she spun around on her toe and stuck her foot out at a quarter to twelve. The king let out a guffaw of approval . . . . and he said, "Sis, you're sure a peach. You're the limit. You can have anything you want." [8]

As Sunday always said, "There'll be in my sermons good fodder, and rock salt, barbed wire and dynamite." [9] No measure was too strong to wipe out sin. Those who objected to this swinging razzle-dazzle were neatly categorized by Sunday's observation that the devil didn't like his methods either. [10]

Ives created the psychological experience of revivalism by using vernacular materials to which he knew the audience would respond. He not only used tunes with a known emotional impact, but he used the same kind of abrupt changes of mood that revival preachers used to excite their listeners. In the third movement of *String Quartet No. 1*, subtitled "A Revival Service," he changed the key four times and the dynamic markings every five bars. In his most famous revival song, "General William Booth Enters Heaven," he abruptly changes the mood and the key at the "B" section beginning "Jesus came to the courthouse door." [11] The previous part has built up to a climax of religious frenzy, with wild syncopation and dissonance. Then, with a sudden hush, the mood changes.

The psychological experience of the revivalist was a familiar experience drawn from the popular culture. The revival preacher used colloquial language that would reach his largely uneducated audience, with homely examples and parables which they would understand and respond to emotionally. He expressed his views of God vividly. His was not the incomprehensible and cold God of the Calvinists, but a hot-blooded Jehovah who wanted his sinners saved NOW. Ives also used musical colloquialisms. The *First Piano Sonata* is typical in its frequent use of hymn-tune material. Among the hymns quoted in this work are "Where's My Wandering Boy Tonight," "I Was a Wandering Sheep," "Bringing in the Sheaves" and "What a Friend We Have in Jesus." The fourth movement of *The First Quartet* is based on the militant "Stand up, Stand up for Jesus!" while the *Second Violin Sonata* uses "Shall We Gather at the River?"

Ives is an expert at using old musical language in new places and in new ways: at the appearance of Jesus in "General William Booth Enters Heaven" the vocal line moves in triplets between C flat, B flat, and A flat over the tonic and subdominant. In this song, Ives' use of vernacular materials is similar to the revivalist's use of verbal vernacular. He heightens the impression of independent action by changing tempo frequently while his use of dissonance, polyrhythms, independent voices, and dynamic markings recreate the heart of the gospeller's experience of confusion and emotionalism.

The form and structure of much of Ives' music reflects the revivalists' emphasis on individual action. Revival preachers emphasized the individual. The first step to a reformed society was the regenerated personality of the individual, and each individual was encouraged to express his religion in his own way. Each man's sins and salvation were of paramount importance. Ives transcribed these values in his music by letting every section of instruments in the *Fourth Symphony* retain its own rhythm, key, and note values. Nothing matches, nor is it intended to; patterns of independent voicing continue throughout the work.

Ives' mixture of sacred and secular tunes, particularly in the *Fourth Symphony*, reflected a Billy Sunday revival. At a typical Sunday revival the trombone and piano background to the choir

singing approached the jazzy. Homer Rodeheaver, Sunday's song
leader, loved musical gimmicks. Rody often had the first rows
antiphonally responding with alternate lines to the chorus sung
by those in the back, the sopranos singing wordless scales while
the tenors sang the melody, the men imitating a steam whistle
and the children repeating some phrase over and over like the
beat of horses' hoofs. The songs were not only good old gospel
hymns, but included such secular favorites as "I've Been Working
on the Railroad," if the presence of some group made them appropriate. It was a performance that brought the revival solidly into
the camp of the "pep" rally and the political convention. When
college students came in a body, they were sure to hear their alma
mater or a football "fight" song—Rody sometimes even called for
a cheer! [12] So when Ives' juxtaposes "Jesus, Lover of My Soul"
with "Yankee Doodle", he is correctly imitating a revival.

The great religious awakening between 1875 and 1915 which
caught the spirit of the progressives and profoundly affected the
thought and music of Charles Ives also produced liberal Protestantism and the Social Gospel movement. Its central idea—socializ-
ing and ethicizing the Protestant religion—permeated American
thought and became a national religious and social goal. Ives,
through his Essays, showed that he adopted the goals of this movement. One of the best approaches to Ives' political, social, and
esthetic thought is through a consideration of this Social Christianity, for it is at the root of "The Majority," Ives' plan for more
direct national government in the United States, and Ives' utopian
dreams such as his planned "Universe Symphony."

The roots of this Social Christianity first sprouted in the particular sect of Protestantism called Unitarianism. Unitarianism was
liberal, ethical, and stressed the dignity and possibility of man
and the importance of the present life. Transcendentalism, an
offshoot of Unitarianism, stressed moral idealism, and through such
experiments as Brook Farm, the application of the teachings of
Jesus and the total message of Christian salvation to society, the
economic life, and social institutions. Although the first great concern of Social Christianity was the abolition of slavery, once this
was an accomplished fact, the religious consciousness directed itself
to the ills of the new industrial civilization and reform.

This growth of Social Christianity called "progressive ortho-
doxy" or "new theology" in the 1880's, developed from "enlight-

ened" conservatives of conventional Protestantism such as Washington Gladden and George D. Herron. To such men, God was at work redeeming society and making His kingdom on earth, and they, along with many of the clergy in the 90's, found that socialism contained a great deal of good. "Christianized Socialism" became a goal to an age believing in evolution, an organic society, and social salvation. Social sacrifice was necessary because the present order of things was wicked and doomed. Every man was a child of God and consequently of infinite worth; the summary of Jesus' teaching was thought to be the Sermon on the Mount. From such ideas as the Kingdom of God on Earth developed a formulation of a social creed and the utilization of the techniques of social service and social welfare activity in American life. In a sense, the progressive movement and the social gospel were really one movement in which the secular and the sacred were mixed. The general characteristics of Social Christianity involved, first, a dominant ethical strain and emphasis placed on the realization of the Kingdom ideal in the present world; second, a realistic appraisal of religion's task; third, a new and realistic view of sin in terms of the implications of a solidaristic society whose members were responsible for its corporate sins. The fourth and most important belief was in progress. A missionary zeal to accomplish this progress was a fifth characteristic that gave a note of crisis and a sense of urgency to Social Christianity. The whole movement, in short, attempted the formation of the law of love in terms equal to the demands of modern society.[13]

Ives found in religion the key for his revolutionary development. The ten settings of Psalms Ives composed between 1895 and 1900 contain some of his most radical experiments, and they are remarkable for their innovations. *Psalm 54* ("Save me, O God, by thy name, and judge me by thy strength") written about 1896, contains augmented chords in the first section (sung by treble voices) while the melody sung by the men is based on the whole-tone scale. *Psalm 25* ("Unto thee, O Lord, do I lift up my soul"), written when Ives was a junior at Yale (1897), contains a twelve-tone row, sung by the choir for four verses. *Psalm 90, Psalm 100,* and *Psalm 150* contain tone clusters, while *Psalm 135* ("Praise Ye the Lord"), written in 1899 or 1900, contains the extremely difficult rhythmic problem of a tympany in 4/4 time against the chorus in 5/4 time.[14] Dr. Edward Griggs, minister for the New Haven Church on the

Green and an old friend of Charles' father, allowed Ives to use his compositions of *Psalm 100, Psalm 150,* and *Psalm 67* in the church, an event that probably startled the congregation.

Yet Ives' music showed the working out of a sincere and conventional religious feeling, however unconventional its expression might be. The assimilation of hymn tunes in Ives' compositions indicates the character of much of his music. John Kirkpatrick's "Index of Tunes" quoted by Ives in his music includes over fifty different hymn tunes. The first movement of the *Third Symphony,* for example, has a section marked Adagio Cantabile, based on the hymn "What a Friend We Have in Jesus" and "There is a Fountain Filled with Blood." "Just As I Am Without One Plea" is the main theme in the third movement. Often snatches of other hymn tunes or suggestions of hymns crop up in Ives' compositions. Some of the themes in the *Second Symphony,* for example, suggest Gospel hymns. Many of his other incidental pieces and almost all of his choral works end with a reference to God. "The Collection," for example, uses a series of chords often found at the end of a hymn. (See Ex. 26) When a performer plays these cadences

Ives, "The Collection".

EXAMPLE 26. Ives. *114 Songs* (privately printed).

many people remember the church and Sundays of long ago. This is a musical reference to the human world embodied in the formal elements of musical art. The hymns are, in effect, symbols of Ives' spiritual acceptance, for the subject of much of Ives' music is his religion, and the working out of that religion of love and intelligence. Yet in this music, Ives attempts to reconcile a Puritan New England view of religion with his own extremely isolated spiritual experiences. The prerogative of the listener is to set aside his own stereotyped views of what church music should sound like, and enter into the spirit of the music of Charles Ives, a highly sensitive, cultured man with a private universe of moral feeling.

Ives identified himself with the movement of social Christianity because he viewed society as making a meaningful progression towards "the good life" and not as a facade masking the ineptitude, cruelty, and avarice of man. Then, too, the desire to eliminate inequities and injustices gripped the country as a whole. The goals were clearly established and would be realized as an essential part of the evolutionary cultural process. According to the theory, man was slowly and inevitably progressing toward a beautiful and rational world free of sin and sham. This Christian doctrine or social gospel combined with the evolutionary theories of Darwin to produce a theory of progress in human affairs. As Ives wrote in the *Essays:*

> . . . There is an "oracle" at the beginning of the *Fifth Symphony;* in those four notes lies one of Beethoven's greatest messages. We would place its translation above the relentlessness of fate knocking at the door, above the spiritual message of Emerson's revelations, even to the "common heart" of Concord—the soul of humanity knocking at the door of the divine mysteries, radiant in the faith that it will be opened—and the human become the divine!" [15]

The progress ultimately aimed at a utopian state of Christian socialism whose chief points were its democratic ideals, its communistic features, and its religious basis. The progress of science led to humanistic daydreaming about welfare states with an unusually high level of culture. These daydreams were often realized, if not in actuality, at least in novels. One study lists forty-eight titles of Utopian romances written between 1884 and 1900.[16] Such utopianism provided some control over rapid social change and helped many to accept change in an age of confusion since it made

change appear meaningful: the transformation of present-day society into a rational and planned one in which inequality and
injustice have disappeared through the realization of spiritual ideas.

The most famous of the welfare-state utopias was *Looking
Backward* by Edward Bellamy, published in 1888. Bellamy's hold
on the later nineteenth century's imagination was based on the
Messianic concept of social transformation. The essential idea of
this concept was that man, by his own efforts to attain enlighten-
ment within historical time could attain brotherhood, a new union,
and a new harmony with nature. Utopia in this sense meant the
ability to plan and change human society, to build a new "good"
society with reason and science.

Such notions of millennial progress with its startling inter-
mingling of mysticism and materialism were the result of what
Henry George called "hopeful fatalism"—the desire for a
catastrophe or apocalyptic revolution. Many predictions of apocalyptic revolution occurred from the seventies onward, giving rise
to millennial hopes and expectations.[17] Many of the people in such
an anxiety-ridden age sought comfort in the supernatural, and faith
healers, mind curers, and mediums were ubiquitous. At the same
time, a number of philosophers, historians, and social scientists
rejected traditional systems of absolutes and followed the lead of
physical scientists and physicists whose declaration of life was
basically open-ended, experimental, and self-determining. All these
changes in intellectual assumptions that brought confusions and
fragmentation led many people to seize upon utopian visions as
a panacea for potential unification.[18]

Ives' music reflected his concern with the ideal of progress
and social utopia. Songs such as "An Election," "Paracelsus," and
"The Majority" present a philosophical statement. The *Essays Before
a Sonata* written to accompany *The Concord Sonata* partially involved
the problem of establishing utopia on earth—the "hog-mind" of
the minority was selfish and feared to believe in the innate goodness
of mankind, the universal mind, the majority. Ives uses one of
his songs to make such political commentary, and then he proceeds
to comment on that. *Nov. 2, 1920*, is the soliloquy of an old man
whose son lies in Flander's Fields. It is the day after the election
and he is sitting by the roadside looking down the valley towards
the station:

. . . Some men and women got tired of a big job; but, over there our men did not quit. They fought and died that better things might be! Perhaps some who stayed at home are beginning to forget and to quit. The pocket book and certain little things talked loud and noble, and got in the way. Too many readers go by the headlines, party men will muddle up the facts, so a good many citizens voted as grandpa always did, or thought a change for the sake of change seemed natural enough.

"It's raining, let's throw out the weather man. Kick him out! Kick him out! Kick him! Prejudice and politics, and the stand-patters came in strong, and yelled "slide back! Now you're safe, that's the easy way!" Then the timid smiled and looked relieved, "We've got enough to eat, to Hell with ideals!"

All the old women, male and female, had their day today, and the hog heart came out of his hole. But he won't stay out long, God always drives him back! O Captain, my Captain! A heritage we've thrown away. But we'll find it again, my Captain, Captain, O my Captain!" [19]

In his note at the end of this song Ives remarks that the voice of the people "sounding through the mouth of the parties, becomes somewhat emasculated. It is not inconceivable that practical ways may be found for more accurately registering and expressing popular thought . . ." He then suggests that if the reader is interested, that he write to Ives and get Ives' plan for a constitutional amendment to rectify the situation.

The Universe Symphony was the culminating expression of Ives' belief in the progress and ultimate victory of mankind. There are about sixty-five pages of *Universe Symphony* fragments, or "patches" which outline chord systems, and in one place, twenty-four different chordal scales. Ives had planned for each continent to have its own wide chord of intervals. Although the work never proceeded beyond this sketch, Ives left a plan on an old manuscript.

Plan for a Universe Symphony
  1. Formation of the countries and mountains
  2. Evolution in nature and humanity
  3. The rise of all to the spiritual

It is unfinished, and intentionally so, for Ives wanted it to be the culminating expression of "music of the ideas". As did the literary realists, Ives used symbolism to stand for an underlying and important reality.[20] The symbols, while part of the event, serve to recall the representing cause. In this case, the music as a whole is symbolic, and as Edward Lippman points out, "The symbolism based on pattern seems capable of representing not only a wider range of objects and happenings, but also of representing ideas themselves. It does this by exemplifying the structural characteristic that an idea embodies: lack of order, for example, or speed, or three-ness." [21]

Ives seems to have had this idea in mind when he began his *Universe Symphony.* He was trying for a parallel way of listening to music suggested by looking at a view, and the idea occurred to him in the Keen Valley on the Plateau in 1915 that the eye saw in two parts.[22] That is, the eyes in looking at the sky saw the foreground subjectively, and when the focus of the vision was changed to the earth and land, they saw the sky subjectively. Ives intended to give an interpretation of this by giving a musical piece in two parts, but both played at the same time, and the whole played through twice; first when the listener focuses his ears on the lower, or earth music, and the second time when he focuses on the upper, or heaven's music.

Ives said that lines, starting at different points and at different intervals, represented the earth part, while the pulse of the universe's life beat was by the percussion orchestra, who were to play their entire movement before any of the other orchestras played. A kind of uneven and interlapping counterpoint, sometimes reaching nine or ten different lines, represented the ledges, rocks, and land formations. A few instruments playing masses of chords built around intervals in each line represented the body of the earth where the rocks, trees, and mountains arise. To represent the atmosphere between earth and heaven, Ives left a vacant space of four tones between B-natural and E-natural. The part of the orchestra representing Heaven had its own chord system and used chordal counterpoint. The earth and heaven groups came into relation harmonically only in cycles, "that is, they go around their own orbit and come to meet each other only where their circles eclipse." [23]

Many of Ives' other works showed facets of man's relation to God. Spiritual introspection, long a part of the good Puritan's heritage, flourished. This psychological tradition of self-revelation was a vital part of Transcendentalism, and the search itself (not its resolution) would later form the foundations of pragmatism.

The inward submersion to survey the limits of identity was also a theme of Walt Whitman, whom Ives greatly admired, and Ives through his song "Walt Whitman" reveals this spiritual quest as assertive and masculine. (See Ex. 27) Ives originally wrote "Walt Whitman" for chorus and chamber orchestra, and in 1921 transcribed it for voice and piano. The verse comes from the twentieth stanza of Whitman's *Song of Myself.* Whitman's vigorous depiction of man as an archetype is a revelation of optimism and the possibilities of progress. With the notion that the superiority of the archetypal figure lay in its representativeness, Whitman led into the democratic aesthetic. In Ives' piece, however, part of the effect lies in the open quality of the parallel fifths and the polychords. As chords lacking a third, they are incomplete, and in their way as wayward as Whitman's *Specimen Days.*

EXAMPLE 27. Ives. "Walt Whitman." Copyright 1933, Merion Music. Used by permission of the publisher.

In contrast with "Walt Whitman" is Ives' song "Like a Sick Eagle" written in 1921 for voice and piano from the chamber ensemble of 1908. (See Ex. 28) Ives' belief is divided. Without a doubt, this song reveals that Ives has by this time realized that the self has evaded his search and utopia had become the war-cry of "Make the world safe for Democracy!" "Like a Sick Eagle" with its quarter-tones, is almost psychopathic, and produces in the listener unease and a "sick" impression. Tragically alien, Ives knew, in the end, the disparity between possibility and reality.

* This part in the score was played by violin and a slide was made down or up through a quartertone, in a semitone interval and through two or three lesser tones in a whole tone interval, except between the last five notes. The voice may do similarly.

EXAMPLE 28. Ives. "Like a Sick Eagle." Copyright 1933, Merion Music. Used by permission of the publisher. Last lines of song.

Man's own concern with the material comforts of his fellow man and his belief in promise and progress suggested a kind of convergence of capitalism, communism, and socialism. At the same time, one of the men who provided political leadership for the progressive movement, Woodrow Wilson, assured the people that their past values were still important. No, he assured the people, he was no radical who "pulls up the roots to see if the thing is growing." A true radical, he maintained, "goes down to the roots to see if the soil is wholesome and that the tap-root is getting the pure nutriment that ought to come from the soil. That is the kind of radicalism I believe in; recultivation, thence reformation of the whole process." [24] Woodrow Wilson also spoke out for representation by all the people as against rule by a class "which imagined itself the guardians of the country's welfare." [25] In the last years of his administration, he tried to blend national unity and private profits, service, manifest destiny and dollar diplomacy. It was all part of a widely held belief that society could be transformed into a rational, beautiful, state of justice and equality by recasting economics according to a few primitivistic rules.

Ives' entrance into the life insurance business after his graduation from Yale was partially the result of his belief that one could sense the organic and primal laws underlying all progress, especially in the social and economic realm. Life insurance appeared to be the best opportunity to do the most good for the largest number of people. In 1907 he and Julian Myrick formed a partnership and secured a general agency with the Washington Life Insurance Company of New York, and in 1910 Ives' agency established a training school for agents. Ives' pamphlet, *The Amount to Carry: Measuring the Prospect* was intended as a handbook for the agents, but the first three sections outline a kind of social history of insurance along Transcendental lines. Ives believed in progress, and for Ives, life insurance was one of the scientific businesses that helped progress along.

Applying the same kind of utopian reasoning to politics that he used in life insurance, Ives decided that the people, the Majority, could decide instinctively what was right for themselves if the fundamental premises were universally available to the greatest number of minds. The problem was that the minority, the politicians, often came between the people and the truth with their own personal prejudices. He proposed, therefore, a ballot in which any citizen could suggest issues which he thought were important. Congress would then categorize these suggestions, and issues mentioned by the greatest number of people would be placed on a ballot containing a complete argument for each side of each issue. All the people would then vote on the issues, and they would be right, because Ives believed in the natural law that if enough minds were able to observe the fundamental truths and facts, the instinctive reasoning of the masses would decide the correct course for the nation. Progress would result because . . . "God is on the side of the majority (the people) . . ." [26] Ives firmly believed that the majority, the people, needed no intermediary. "Governments will pass from the representative to the direct," he wrote.[27] Utopia was just ahead, reasoned Ives:

> . . . the day of leaders, as such, is gradually closing—the people are beginning to lead themselves—the public store of reason is slowly being opened—the common universal mind and the common over-soul is slowly but inevitably coming into its own.[28]

Seeking political reform to hurry the day when utopia would arrive on the American scene, Ives' paper, *The Majority,* begun about 1912 and finished about 1922, showed specific ways in which the nation could operate in accordance with the natural law of Emerson. Like the other men of his time, Ives was giving deep thought to the inequities of capitalism and the utopian ideas of Christian socialism. He was deeply concerned with the problems of economic security in a "society clogged up with unnatural economic arrangements." [29] His solution combined the good points of both communism and capitalism, for he proposed a system in which each individual would be limited to a maximum annual income of $7500 and be given $900 as a starter towards making that maximum.

He also formulated some notes on which he called a "People's World Union", a kind of United States of the World, under whose constitution each country would live its own life. This utopian dream of a government limited to no national boundaries was held in common with Woodrow Wilson, whose League of Nations proved equally impractical. "The government of the world I live in is not framed in after-dinner conversation around a table in a capital city," wrote Ives, "for there is no capital—a government of principles not parties; of a few fundamental truths and not of many political expediencies—a government conducted by virtuous leaders, for it will be led by all, for all are virtuous, as then their "innate virtue" will no more be perverted by unnatural institutions." [30]

Peace was linked with the coming of the kingdom of God in the inevitable upward evolution. Ives exemplified the great majority of Americans who combined the belief in the supreme importance of the individual's relation to God (revival/fundamentalism) with a belief in the gradual, universal improvement of society by men's own efforts.[31]

Religion was a vital force in Charles Ives' life. The camp meetings Ives remembered from his youth made a vivid impression on him, and he often "reasserted" the old-time religion and the revivals in his music. The emotionalism and the individualism of revivals found their way in certain pieces Ives wrote, while in others, such as *General William Booth Enters Heaven,* Ives directly imitated the revival preacher's rhetoric, its rise and fall, and tempo change. Ives' use of the vernacular and snatches of popular tunes also paralleled the use of slang of the saw-dust trail preachers.

Aside from revivalism, a deep religiosity permeated most of Ives' music. His realism contained a fundamental moral orientation and his beliefs were a combination of the fundamental individualism à la Emerson's *Self-Reliance* and the progressive utopianism of the Social Gospel. Ives combined the theology of the former and the economic theory of the latter in his political and social thought. *The Majority,* for example, illustrated the fundamentalists' cry for self-expression and self-development and the belief of the Social Gospel in a coming utopia. Although Ives' music was not recognized in its own time, it often embodied accurately the cultural pattern of his era.

6

THE MIDDLE-CLASS CONSCIENCE: PRAGMATISM

T HE REALISTS TOOK ONE EASY STEP FROM substance to process. As Harold Kolb points out, the realists used pragmatic concepts in their fiction long before Charles Sanders Peirce published his theory.[1] Huck Finn says characteristically:

> . . . And as for me, I don't care shucks for the morality of it, nohow. When I start in to steal a nigger, or a watermelon, or a Sunday school book, I ain't no ways particular how it's done. What I want is my nigger; or what I want is my watermelon; or what I want is my Sunday school book; and if a pick's the handiest thing, that's the thing I'm agoing to dig that nigger or that watermelon or that Sunday school book out with; and I don't give a dead rat what the authorities thinks about it nuther.[2]

Adapting to the circumstances is Huck's by-word, and his unconscious use of pragmatism is typical of the realists. Their commitment to relativity and multiplicity more than hinted at pragmatic theory and experience as a basis for action.

The experimental theory of knowledge owed its prevalence in part to earlier Darwinian theories. The climate of opinion was due, in part, to the rapid social change of American society. Industrialization, urbanization, the laws of thermodynamics, the growth and mergers of railroads and industry were responsible for the correlated transfer from absolutes to experiments as a dependable source of knowledge. In many respects, the theory of evolution reinforced, and was reinforced by, the work of Pierre Janet, Morton Prince, and Sigmund Freud. Anthropology, social psychology,

comparative religion, folklore, institutional and historical economics, and the "new" history were disciplines that arose in the late
nineteenth and early twentieth century that complemented the
idea of method rather than authority as the principal resource of
intellectual life.

Charles Sanders Peirce, in a thoroughly Darwinian manner,
used the concepts of universal random variation and selection to
suggest a statistical approach to aggregates of phenomena. Proba-
bilities replaced the causal determinism of older logic, and chance
left the individual partially undetermined as to the laws of its
behavior. This, in effect, freed the individual from the restraints
imposed upon him by the Social Darwinists, who had clung to
an absolutist conception of environment in which the environment
posed selective standards against which organic and human characteristics and behavior were to be measured.[3]

Herbert Spencer, whose application of evolution to society gave
him a public influence that transcended Darwin's, assumed the
environment as a fixed norm. For the pragmatists, change was
the only constant, and the environment was something that could
be manipulated. Pragmatism, an application of evolutionary biology to human ideas, emphasized the study of ideas as instruments
of the organism.[4] All evolutionists, as Stow Persons points out, have
a characteristic sense of reality as an ongoing process, and thus
a similar consciousness of the relationship between past, present,
and future. But the Darwinian brand of evolution had the effect
of destroying an authoritative past independent of its present uses.[5]

The affiliation of pragmatism with the theory of evolution
is thus apparent in an exposition of the doctrine.[6] The role of
experience as confirmation or disconfirmation, not origination, was
suggestive of the process of natural selection and survival of the
fittest.[7] It was an old way of thinking, and William James pointed
out the parallels between the facts of social evolution and of zoo-
logical evolution as expounded by Darwin.[8]

James' recognition of the kinship between pragmatism and
evolution clarifies the subject: how the fluid state of knowledge
known as pragmatism, a virtual cultural underground, crystallized
into a tool that Charles Ives used to carry his art into astonishing
innovation and renewal of old ideas.[9]

Ives was not alone in his readjustment of formal values. The
same influences that gave form and direction to his music over-

flowed in progressive politics, art, literature, and the social gospel that preached a coming utopia for mankind. The revealing title of Edward Bellamy's utopian novel, *Looking Backward,* in more ways than one describes a period "whose backward looks were for the sake of forward looks." [10] The chief change was in the idea of experience, which traditionally referred ideas back to the experiences of the past. The pragmatists, instead, referred theoretical constructions to the future with the inevitable question of "What difference will it make if. . . ." George Santayana called it "that strange pragmatic reduction of yesterday to tomorrow" and suggested that "the backward perspective of time is perhaps really an inverted expectation." [11]

Not the least merit of this conception was its rejection of fixed principles, closed systems, pretended absolutes, dogma, artificiality, and the pretense of finality in truth. This rejection takes various forms: the conception of ideas as plans of action; the experimental conception of knowing as itself involving doing; the denial of immediate knowledge; the distinguishing of knowledge from immediate experiences often confused with it; and the discrediting of the notion of knowledge as a disclosure of antecedent reality.[12] These marginal philosophical theories emerge slowly in their proper perspective, for they are generally considered as rhetoric having no connection with Ives' musical talents. The truth lies somewhere between. Ives' prose is unusual in its penetrating relevance to the American scene that produced these theories, and certain parts of his music provide a pungent comment that rounds out the theory.

"Pragmatism" in Ives is only a very general term, intended to show the philosophic tendencies within the period, the general social and intellectual influences to which Ives was in varying degrees subject. The emphasis in this thesis is on continuities, common influences, and common traits, and for this reason a digression into the unique or emphatic in Peirce and James is not relevant. Ives' connection to the pragmatic movement was chiefly through Emerson.

Many scholars have documented the pragmatic ideas of Emerson.[13] "Historically, the year 1871 first saw the transformation of Transcendentalism into pragmatism," wrote Frederick Carpenter in a recent study of Emerson's ideas.[14] Later pragmatists developed and applied Emerson's insights and left written statements of their philosophic indebtedness. Remarks of Charles S. Peirce and Oliver

W. Holmes, marginal notations of William James in two volumes of Emerson's essays, and the essays on Emerson by John Dewey show that Emerson was a precursor of pragmatism. An early study of Emerson's philosophy called it "pragmatic mysticism" while a later study by a social psychologist suggests that Emerson's philosophy foreshadowed the pragmatic thesis.[15]

Although Ives surely absorbed pragmatism from Emerson's philosophy, he was also acquainted with the works of Oliver Wendell Holmes, an active participant in the early formulation of pragmatism who worked out its application to law.[16] According to Howard Boatwright's notes,[17] Ives quoted freely from the works of Holmes and may have realized that Holmes' predictive theory of law and the experimental theory of knowledge owed their prevalence in part to Darwinian analogies. Future experiment (method) was what tested a hypothesis, not past authority. Holmes, moreover, had read William James's *Psychology* in 1890, "every word of it," he said, "with delight and admiration." [18] James based much of his theory of the mind's attention span on the writings of Hermann Helmholtz,[19] whose works were familiar to Ives.[20] Ives thus could have absorbed his pragmatism from any of several sources.

The difference that pragmatism made in Ives' music appeared first in his rejection of nineteenth century conventional harmonies and forms. With the European music of Romanticism their main model, and with German music as the ideal, Americans wanted their musicians to abide by the rules. This meant that, in essence, a symphony was a fairly predictable affair. The composer stated his themes, tempi, and tonality in the first few minutes. Everyone knew that he would develop these themes in some way, but his skill as a composer would be judged on the subjectivity and ingenuity with which he could vary and develop motives within a framework. The pattern of this framework consisted of certain musical conventionalities—phrases were a certain number of measures, followed by their "answer." The first theme was expected to be in the tonic key, the second in the dominant. First movements were in sonata-allegro form, slow movements were in song-form. Individuality and novelty were valued, but only if they fitted into the slot marked "virtuoso" which carried connotations of lonely, sublime, and Beethovenesque subjectivism laced with a few mildly exotic murmurs and crowned with an arpeggiated chord on the dominant-seventh. The sublime simply had to be serious, and if the composer and/or performer could manage to be consumptive, his music was even more desirable. Music of the nineteenth century was, for many composers, a closed system. Experience referred musical ideas back to musical forms of the past.

As with all pragmatists who looked backwards so they could see forwards, Ives did not ignore the forms of the past. Many of his works were written within so-called classical structures; Ives merely adjusted the meaning to an extraordinary degree. Even in an early work like the *First Symphony* he modulates rapidly and widely; the original draft shows the first theme passing through eight different keys. Another early work (1897) *Organ Prelude and Postlude for a Thanksgiving Service* begins with a polychord, C minor and D minor, followed by chords generally a tone apart, major and minor together.

Ives' rejection of set musical conventionalities used within classical forms often took him into experimenting sheerly for the sake of experiment. The *Second Piano Sonata* is written almost entirely without a meter signature, except for scattered measures in the first and third movements. Ives places the barlines seemingly more as a visual aid than to establish a beat. This lack of a meter signature and the implication of an open-ended universe demands that one experiment to create his own phrase patterns according to his inner view. An old formal substance dissolves to a process. "Experience," William James wrote, "has no such inner duplicity; and the separation of it into consciousness and content comes, not by way of subtraction, but by way of addition—the addition, to a given concrete piece of it, of other sets of experiences, in connection with which severally its use of function may be of two different kinds." [21] Ives accordingly indicates that the performer may add notes, or vary the dynamics or interpretation from performance to performance. (See Ex. 29) Change, experiment, and motion are the meaning, rather than a formal harmonic progression or melody moving through time. There are other trivial features of Ives' music that take on significance in this context. The *Second Piano Sonata* contains passages to be played with the clenched fist. (See Ex. 30) Far from being a mere trick, this use illustrates a principal pragmatic resource—rescuing ideas from absolutes by experimentalism. A musical idea whose performance involves more fingers than performers normally have, shows up on the page with the notation that the performer should use a "strip of board 14¾ ins.

1. For the most part, this movement is supposed to be played as fast as possible, lightly and not literally. Marks of tempo, ex - pression, etc. are use as little as possible. If the score itself, the preface or an interest in Hawthorne suggest nothing, marks will only make things worse. 2 It is not intended that the relation 2:1. between the 32nd & 16th notes here, be held to literally, 3. The use of both pedals is almost constantly required.

EXAMPLE 29. Ives. *Second Pianoforte Sonata.* Copyright by Associated Music Publishers. Used by permission. P. 21, measure 1.

long and heavy enough to press the keys down without striking." (See Ex. 31) Ives makes his meaning quite clear when he writes:

> In fact, these notes, marks, and near pictures of sounds etc., are in a kind of way a platform for the player to make his speeches on. And as I tried to infer in the book, in various places, that Emerson, Thoreau especially, and the others perhaps less so weren't static, rule-making, do-as-I'm-told professors,—to me their thoughts, substance, and inspiration change and grow, rise to this mountain, then to that, as the years go on through time to the Eternities.

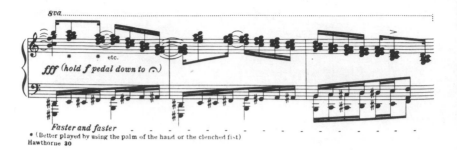

EXAMPLE 30. Ives. *Second Pianoforte Sonata*, "Concord." Copyright by Associated Music Publishers. Used by permission. P. 40, measures 7, 8, 9.

> It was the attempt to catch this, to give one man's impression, reflected as it might be through sounds—inadequate enough probably to others—but to not let music get the best of it, of them or the ideals. If the music is just taken as such, and by itself, it shouldn't mean the right something or anything much—at least I hope not!—if it does, then it would show that my theory was all wrong—or rather I might say, if it were not for my years of friendship with Emerson, Alcott, Thoreau, and Hawthorne, the music, whatever it is, wouldn't be whatever it is!" [22]

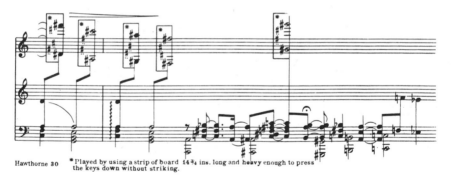

EXAMPLE 31. Ives. *Second Pianoforte Sonata*, "Concord." Copyright by Associated Music Publishers. Used by permission. P. 25, measures 12, 13.

The scope of experiment in the music of Ives comprises two parts. The first of these is a kind of "pure" experiment with little or no attempt to intrude a meaning on the musical statement. These experiments are stylistic. More complicated and elaborate are his experiments with accumulations of musical ideas of varying spatial and temporal orders of complexity. (See Ex. 32) Some pages

EXAMPLE 32. Ives. *The Anti-Abolitionist Riots in Boston in the 1850's.* Copyright 1949, Mercury Music. Used by permission of the
publisher. P. 40.

from "Lincoln the Great Commoner" show the kind of overlapping
of phrases and motives (that is, some end or break while others
are continuing or beginning) that illustrates this kind of accumulation of images. (See Ex. 33)

Ives was preoccupied with the question of what the rational
mind could do when common-place "things" were considered as

EXAMPLE 33. Ives, "Lincoln the Great Commoner." Copyright 1959, Merion Music, Inc. Used by permission of the publisher. P. 9. This example illustrates use of a recitative like statement ". . . wrenching rafters from their ancient hold" and the use of dissonance and chord clusters, as well as text-painting.

imaginative reality. The objects of our consciousness, after all, contribute to the musical content and certainly the evidence points to the fact that Ives considered titles to be more than just titles: "Slugging a Vampire," "Where the Eagle," "The Celestial Country," "The Unanswered Question." The key was the accessibility to experience; ideas become plans of action. Titles, or the ideas in titles, elicit from the listener a reaction, and the reaction due to ideas and memories is in many cases as strong as that due to sensible presences. William James, a great believer in the reality of the unseen, thought that in many cases the material sensations actually present would have a weaker influence on our action than ideas of remoter facts.[23]

The sine qua non for Ives is not to violate the integrity of music as a subjective idea. He accepts the contradiction inherent in this idea, this denial of immediate knowledge, and in doing so becomes a man with a message but no medium. The pragmatic belief that knowledge does not necessarily disclose antecedent reality thus rears its head. The absolute conformity of facts to law was, for both Ives and Charles Sanders Peirce, an assumption which did not rest on empirical evidence, whereas that of chance of spontaneous departures from law did. Peirce believed that ideas spread, acquired feeling and became general, merging in a continuum of mind. His theory is that the world is full of partial stories that run parallel to one another, beginning and ending at odd times. These stories mutually interlace and interfere at points, and are difficult to unify completely in our minds. Ives juxtaposes many themes in his music in different instruments so that they do exactly this (cf. *Three Places in New England* and *The Robert Browning Overture*). Ives' piano piece, *The Anti-Abolitionist Riots in Boston in the 1850's* shows, in the second system, a complex rhythmic relation on three levels. Different melodic ideas interlace, perhaps in the same way that Peirce's thoughts and "stories" mutually interlace and run parallel to one another, beginning and ending at different points.

Another one of Peirce's theories is that our fundamental ways of thinking about things are discoveries of exceedingly remote ancestors, which have been able to preserve themselves throughout the experience of all subsequent time. This idea, of course, related pragmatism both to the theory of evolution and what Santayana called "the reduction of yesterday to tomorrow." Peirce decided that the way in which an individual settles into new opinions is by grafting them upon the ancient stock of old opinions with a minimum of disturbance:

> As for that part of the Past that lies beyond memory, the Pragmaticist doctrine is that the meaning of its being believed to be in connection with the Past consists in the acceptance as truth of the conception that we ought to conduct ourselves according to it (like the meaning of any other belief). Thus, a belief that Christopher Columbus discovered America really refers to the future.[24]

Ives more than matches this ambiguous issue by grafting some of his most radical musical "opinions" onto old tune sources. Strange, exotic new harmonies or dissonances, conglomerate rhythms and new sprouts of melody often start from an old tune. Ives' music, which so often looked backward as it progressed, paralleled William James' definition for pragmatism, "a new name for some old ways of thinking." Form ceases to be an ordering in time, and as Peirce remarks, "Whatever exists, really acts upon other existents, and so obtains a self-identity, and is definitely individual." [25]

Ives' music is filled with submerged scenes. Many of his pieces have a fragmented appearance, caused by rapidly changing points of view and a suspiciously omniscient focus of innocence enmeshed in a web of experience. "There may be an analogy," wrote Ives, "between both the state and power of artistic perceptions and the law of perpetual change, that ever-flowing stream, partly biological, partly cosmic, ever going on in ourselves, in nature, in all life." [26] From this Ives seems to deduce that "events", not "particles" must be the "stuff" of music. What has been thought of as a kind of musical absolute (for example, a musical phrase that starts somewhere and goes somewhere) is now to be thought of as a series of events. The series of events that replace the musical absolute is experiences or image processes that succeed each other, not necessarily because of the process of the music, but because of the associations in the mind of the listener between the images themselves.[27] A chain reaction occurs when the mind establishes the connection between the immediate sound of the present and moments of the past. The result is a continuity of past with present. This principle of continuity excludes the dualism of matter and mind. For this reason, Ives says he is more interested in "the way something happens" rather than in that something itself.

If the rise of the unconscious altered the system of "absolute" knowledge, physics and physiology reinforced the conclusions of the timelessness of the unconscious. Einstein substituted events for particles; each event had to each other a relation called "interval" which could be analyzed in various ways—according to one way, two events might be simultaneous, according to another, one event might be earlier than the other. The choice in interpretation was entirely arbitrary.[28] Matter, according to this theory, is not part of the ultimate material of the world, but just "a convenient way of collecting events into bundles," as Bertrand Russell puts it.

At the same time that physics was asserting that matter was less material and physical phenomena possibly discontinuous, psychology was suggesting something analogous—that the mind was a kind of sieve for ideas rather than a "storehouse." Physics and psychology thus approached each other. While William James' criticism of consciousness was a kind of groping in the dark, it illustrated the characteristic shift in the period, the transfer from substance to process, from matter to method. In such an atmosphere it was natural that Ives should conceive of music as a field for research into the nature of the mind. Ives firmly believed that more and more premises of truth were coming before men, so he disregarded the "authority" of European music and struck out in a direction of his own.[29] His lack of concern with the external realities and hostility toward material things were some of the consequences of viewing consciousness as involvement in a moving world of action and reaction. His emphasis on "the way things happen" was natural in an era dominated by science which conceived of knowledge not as a body of doctrine but as a method of procedure. Pragmatism was a method of procedure that stood for no solutions but only a program for more work, a means in which existing realities could be changed. Since it was essentially nothing new, Ives could take up the method and exploit his experimentalism while keeping his realism on a reservation disguised as transcendentalism. However much his ultimate qualities lie beyond method, method guided his hand always.

In a sense, certain aspects of pragmatism reflected the old transcendental denial of material reality. The stress on "process" and the mind was transcendental, and transcendental thought, in turn, utilized certain oriental concepts and philosophies. The spiritualist stream was running wide at the turn of the century, and the notes of empirical analysis and intellectual prestige added by the sciences of physics and psychology helped to bridge the gap between Eastern and Western philosophy implied by the belief in mind as a continuum.

In support of their interpretations of limitless consciousness, many turned to the first source, the Orient. In 1894 the Boston Metaphysical Club began the second year of its exploration of "man's deeper nature, its development and possibilities" in "an age of divine unrest and inquiry." At the same time Mr. Kehiro Nakemura opened classes in Japanese with references from Percival Lowell, Josiah Royce and William James.[30] The intellectuals and artists all felt the attraction of the East, and the cult of the so-called "Boston Brahmins" grew.

Oriental influences also show up in the music of Ives partially because Transcendentalism, based in part on certain oriental beliefs, was still a vital force to Ives at the turn of the century. Oriental artists are not interested in photographic representation of an object but in interpreting its spirit, for oriental art is cosmocentric. It sees man as an integral part of Nature.[31] Eastern art is contemplative, introvertive, emotional and idealizing—adjectives which seem to describe much of Ives' music fairly well. Certain features in Ives' music, including his use of partials, quarter-tones, subtleties of melody, rhythm, ornamentation and tonal nuances are common in Oriental music. (See Ex. 34) Ives' emphasis on improvisation in parts of his music is parallel to the lack of written sources of Oriental music. This lack is an intrinsic feature of Oriental music whose irrational character forestalls recording in exact symbols.[32]

Many Orientals, with a belief that events are without real significance, naturally do not feel that artists should observe, record, or speak about them accurately. Count Keyserling wrote in his Diary:

> Indians know nothing of history, nor have they any organs for historical truth. Mythology and reality are one and the same thing to them. And thus legend is judged as reality and reality transformed to legend; and every time this happens as if it were a matter of course. . . . They believe everything with the same readiness; they accept what is likely just as they accept what is improbable. . . .

Hindus do not differentiate strictly between fiction and truth, dream and reality, imagination and reality; for this reason it is impossible to rely upon their statements.[33]

Artistic unreality is the core of reality for the Orientalist. One of the philosophers to interpret far Eastern civilization to Westerners, Ernest Fenollosa, wrote that "Relations are more real and more important than the things which they relate." [34] He meant that relations glimpsed as a whole were more alive than each component part.[35]

EXAMPLE 34. Ives. *Symphony No. 4.* Copyright by Associated Music Publishers. Used by permission. P. 16, measures 1, 2, at A (strings only). Certain features in Ives' music, such as the use of quarter-tones, are common in Oriental music.

Riding on the same wave of thought, the pragmatists appeared with their version of truth and relationships. Ideas, they said, (which themselves are but parts of our experience) become true just in so far as they help us to get into satisfactory relation with other parts of our experience, to summarize them and get about among them by conceptual shortcuts instead of following the interminable succession of particular phenomena.[36]

This emphasis on process led to the artist's view of life as a ceaseless flux, as consciously incomplete and experimental—ideas which Ives would later exploit in his music. Yet like most of the intellectual backgrounds of Ives' innovations, the pragmatic method of composing was not new. Pragmatism was inherent in his teacher, Horatio Parker's philosophical position, for he had insisted that the "empirical process" was a composer's only effective guide.[37]

Charles Ives' approach is pragmatic since he is interested in the method, or as he says, "the way things happen." Examples of his reduction of substance to process appear in his musical experiments and stream-of-consciousness technique in which logical musical forms themselves evolve in the continuum. Some of his experiments involve an accumulation of musical ideas that seem to parallel Peirce's writings on the interrelation of ideas. And like Peirce, Ives believed in a theory of cosmic evolution, according to which the world was progressing in a gradual evolutionary manner to an ideal state.

Pragmatism was a refracting medium for many currents in American life, for many conflicting tendencies. It repudiated limiting definitions and consistency, partly because America, at a crisis in its culture, was seeking refuge in its past, in various forms of utopianism and in psychic withdrawal. Many, in a period of critical change, were retreating from the systematization of consciousness. The breakdown of consciousness separated them from stable conditions and many men turned inward, like so many Oriental sages, to seek an awareness, either absent or unacknowledged in their chaotic society.

CONCLUSION: CHARLES IVES AND THE AMERICAN MIND

N O MATTER HOW ORIGINAL A MUSICIAN may be, the nature of the social order circumscribes the development of his inventiveness. Marginal elements within music do not become dominant and coalesce into a style by pure chance or by an ineluctable process; these elements correspond to the social texture of the societies. Almost everyone acknowledges that cultural change, immanent forces, ideas and processes, are responsible for changes in the various arts, and some think that music may reflect social conditions. Yet scholars have, for the most part, carefully skirted the particulars.

The preceding chapters attempt to explore the social psychology of music by choosing key aspects of the subject matter and concentrating on the material and intellectual factors in the social situation that were characteristic of the aspect. Latent factors, other variables, and emotional idiosyncrasies leave many problems unsolved. But this comparative approach clarifies some of the generalized attributes of the creative process and provides a musicological test case that can be applied to other composers.

Ives' extraordinary home environment inspired his devotion to the commonplace and provided the bridge he would later use to build his own recreation of a usable past. With his unusual father he explored acoustics, natural sounds, and new combinations of instruments while absorbing revival hymns, sentimental parlor music, and popular songs from the townspeople of Danbury. Later at Yale he learned European-oriented musical traditions. His teacher, Horatio Parker, concentrated on the disciplinary aspects of music, but at the same time, Parker's philosophy of "form and substance," "strong, masculine music" and his lectures which often reiterated the dogmas of the Transcendentalists had a great influence on Ives' development. Parker's philosophical position was inherently pragmatic, and his work, too, was often a hodge-podge of tunes and stylistic traits borrowed from other composers.

Along with borrowed tunes, Ives borrowed ideas. Most of his so-called avant-garde beliefs in what constitutes music can be traced directly back to Thoreau and the other Transcendentalists. Ives' interest in the psychological aspect of music is a distinguishing feature of the Transcendental impact on art, for most of the Transcendentalists from Margaret Fuller to John Sullivan Dwight were interested in music as a psychological experience. Their shift from objective modes to subjective modes of thought was a forerunner of later realism. The realism of the mind took the form of the stream-of-consciousness technique, with ideas linked in complex chains of associations.

Ives' attempt to create human consciousness in music led him to use tunes which had a prior association in the mind of the listener and certain mechanical controls to represent the movement of consciousness in music; for example, his use of nonmetrical melody interwoven in relatively free temporal relationships. Within his work, the principles of psychological free-association guided him. His musical quotes are psychologically coherent.

Realism also sprang from Transcendentalism because the Transcendentalists believed that the common, the familiar, and the natural were links to a higher spiritual world. Consequently, a study of the familiar, (Nature), would lead to a knowledge of the Absolute, the essence that pervaded all things. Realism, a pluralistic term, appears to have four points: a subject matter chosen from the middle ground, a technique exploring the subjective, exactness and universality of representation, and a fundamental moral orientation. Ives' realism in the choice of subject matter shows his preoccupation with conditions and manners indigenous to America. The realists, agreeing with Emerson's dictum not to seek outside the self, viewed the subconscious as an essential part of reality, and Ives' music depicted this subjectivity with collections of fragments, motifs, scraps, and pieces in tangled masses of details in continuous flux and change. His ambiguous endings of pieces parallel the unresolved endings of realistic novels, while the exactness and universality of representation of his realism assumes the form of quoted tunes. The fundamental moral orientation in Ives consists of his pose of innocence and the sincere and conventional religious feeling conveyed by the hymn tunes and references to God in his music. Ives' emphasis on religion was partly the attempt to deny the normal concept of time. Revival hymns were one means of idealizing the past and escaping from historic time, for nineteenth-century Americans sought escape from time by utopian visions of social felicity, a Messianic concept. The simultaneous visions of the ideal and the real that were recurrent themes of utopia were techniques exploring the subjective, subconscious side of man, a side vitalized by the belief in progress through science.

In believing that science with its method of solving problems could make a utopia, Americans took one easy step from belief in substance to belief in process, and with the belief in process the philosophy of pragmatism was born. Pragmatism, an old way of thinking, owed its prevalence in part to earlier Darwinian theories, a fact that William James pointed out in 1880. Ives, an extremely well-read person, may have realized the implications of pragmatic thought from Oliver W. Holmes, William James, and Hermann L. F. Helmholtz. In any case, his rejection of set musical conventionalities often led him into experimenting sheerly for the sake of experiment, while his belief in the reality of the unseen fixed his earlier Transcendental ideas of music as an idea and not sound itself.

"There may be an analogy," wrote Ives, "between both the state and power of artistic perceptions and the law of perpetual change, that ever-flowing stream partly biological, partly cosmic, ever going on in ourselves, in nature, in all life." [1] From this Ives seems to deduce that "events" not "particles" must be the "stuff" of music. In the same way, Einstein substituted events for particles; each event had to each other event a relation called "interval" which could be analyzed in various ways. The choice in interpretation was entirely arbitrary. While physics asserted that matter was less material and physical phenomena were possibly discontinuous, psychology was suggesting something analogous. Physiology reinforced the conclusions of the timelessness of the unconscious.

Supporting their interpretations of limitless consciousness implied by the sciences of physics and psychology, many pointed out that the old Transcendental denial of material reality had its first source in the Orient. Relations, in thus becoming more real and important than the things which they relate, bridge the gap between Western pragmatism and Oriental mysticism. Many of the pragmatists' cosmological ideas thus parallel Eastern thought.

Related to the problem of consciousness was the question of the meaning of time and duration in psychology, philosophy, literature, and music. Henri Bergson's *Essay on the Immediate Data of Consciousness* developed distinctions between mechanical and psychological time and argued that time is best exemplified in the overlapping of mental states in man himself. Bergson rejected the idea of time being separated into a "before" and "after" and insisted that only an interrelation of all its moments may properly be considered duration. Pragmatism, in its emphasis on the fluid character of reality, was thus a continuation of Bergsonianism.

If pragmatism, that intellectual implication of Darwinism, dumped on the former blueprints of the universe, it did so with the deliberate naughtiness inherent in declaring intellectual freedom. And if pragmatism, with its element of playfulness, succeeded in making our search for maturity a little less "serious", that, as Gilbert Chase would probably agree, is "all to the good." The search for the sublime, after all, does not have to be completely solemn.

BIBLIOGRAPHY

THE FOLLOWING SELECTED LISTS PROVIDE only the most basic titles relating to the period or movement studied. Some important books found in one section also relate to other sections. The following scheme provides easy reference:

I. PRIMARY

Unpublished Secondary Sources
Secondary Sources

II. GENERAL BACKGROUND, 1874–1920

III. CHARLES IVES AND HIS MUSIC

Books
Articles
Dissertations and Theses
Other

IV. TRANSCENDENTALISM AND RELIGION

V. THE STREAM OF CONSCIOUSNESS

VI. REALISM

VII. PRAGMATISM

I. PRIMARY SOURCES

The chief sources for a study of Charles Ives are, of course, in the library of the Yale School of Music. The papers there total over several thousand pieces. There are about 8,000 pages of music manuscript alone, as well as programs, reviews, and originals of Ives' published works. There is also material relating to the *Concord Sonata,* the political papers *Stand By the President and the People, The Majority,* and the *Twentieth Amendment.* Ives' unpublished story, *George's Adventures or a Study in Money, Coherence, Words and Other Things (A Good Model for a Poor Story)* seems based on ideas from

The Majority. His other short story called *Broadway* (*Not a Continuation of Main Street*) describes the adventures of two different types of agents and was printed by Ives & Myrick from Agency Bulletins of July-September 1922.

Many of Ives' early letters survive: two in 1880, two in 1881, five in 1886, seven in 1889, four in 1890, and forty-four between 1893 and 1894. Included in the file are also letters from Nicolas Slonimsky, John Becker, Elliot Carter, Carl Ruggles, Henry Bellaman, and John Griggs as well as correspondence with insurance businessmen.

The collection also has an assortment of miscellaneous excerpts from newspaper and magazine articles. The sample contains no unfavorable reviews.

Other researchers will be happy to know that Ives' unpublished manuscripts—around six volumes of orchestral work and eleven volumes of other media—are in the process of being microfilmed. In 1968 another project was inaugurated by the music library at Yale to produce an oral history of Ives. To date, thirty people (49 reels of tape) have been interviewed by Vivian Perlis, reference librarian of the Ives Collection, and release by Columbia records is due about 1972.

The collection contains a number of good student papers on Ives. Notable are the senior essay by Ralph J. Moore, Jr. "The Background and the Symbol: Charles E. Ives" (Yale, 1954) and Bentley Layton's "An Introduction to the 114 Songs of Charles Ives" (Harvard B.A. thesis, 1963).

John Kirkpatrick's *A Temporary Mimeographed Catalogue of the Music Manuscripts and Related Materials of Charles Edward Ives, 1874–1954,* given by Mrs. Ives to the library of the School of Music at Yale University is a chronological grouping of scores, sketches and fragments. It is indexed elaborately, so that, for example, it is possible to identify the other pieces a fragment was associated with and the dates of composition. Kirkpatrick has also written some useful introductions to published scores and his *Memos of Charles Ives,* soon to be published by W. W. Norton, is a useful compendium of Ives' writings.

The Essays Before a Sonata and Other Writings by Charles Ives, edited by Howard Boatwright are the most useful source of Ives' published writings. *Charles Ives and His Music,* a biography by Henry and Sidney Cowell covers the basics.

A. UNPUBLISHED SECONDARY SOURCES

The dissertation by Frank Rossiter, "Charles Ives and American Culture: The Process of Development, 1874–1921" (Princeton, 1970) shows Ives as deeply committed to the genteel, middle-class life of his time and social class. Charles W. Ward's Master's thesis (The University of Texas, 1969) "The Use of Hymn Tunes as an Expression of "Substance and Manner" in the Music of Charles Edward Ives 1874–1954" explores in detail Ives' expressions of "substance". Several other theses mostly of musicological interest include: Kenneth Robert Mays, "The Use of Hymn Tunes in the Works of Charles Ives" (Indiana, 1961); Mary Ann Vinquist, "The Psalm Settings of Charles Ives" (Indiana, 1965); Lee Cyril Rosen, "The Violin Sonatas of Charles Ives", (University of Illinois, 1965); Betty Dustin Myers, "The Orchestral Music of Charles Ives" (Indiana, 1951).

"A Charles Ives Primer" by Johannes Riedel and Robert Oudal (University of Minnesota, Minneapolis, 1969) is an excellent introduction to music idioms as found in Charles Ives' music. The primer also contains an excellent bibliography of newspaper and magazine articles, books and recordings, as well as an outline of class topics.

B. SECONDARY SOURCES

There are a flood of articles and monographs on various aspects of the Transcendental movement. The best anthology is Perry Miller, ed. *The Transcendentalists* (Cambridge, 1967) which gives a clear view of the beginnings of the Transcendentalist group and selections from the writings of the chief proponents. Another fairly good source is Myron Simon and Thornton Parsons *Transcendentalism and Its Legacy.* Any biography of Emerson will provide the basic facts. Eduard C. Lindeman's *Basic Selections from Emerson* (N.Y., 1954) is a neat condensation of the voluminous philosopher.

Thoreau's *Journals,* edited by Bradford Torrey (Boston, 1906) and Margaret Fuller, *Memoirs of Margaret Fuller* (Boston, 1851) are good autobiographical studies. By far the best source I found was an unpublished Ph.D. dissertation (University of Minnesota, 1964) by Daniel Rider, "The Musical Thought and Activities of the New England Transcendentalists." This is an excellent compendium of the writings of six Transcendentalists on music.

No study on Transcendentalism could be complete without reading F. O. Matthiessen's *American Renaissance* (N.Y., 1941) and M. H. Abrams' *The Mirror and the Lamp: Romantic Theory and the Critical Tradition* (N.Y., 1958).

The literature on the stream-of-consciousness as a method is difficult to find. The most relevant work is Robert Humphrey, *The Stream of Consciousness in the Modern Novel* (Berkeley, 1955). Development of the consciousness through various psychological thinkers is considered in the dissertations by J. C. Burnham, "Psychoanalysis in American Civilization Before 1918" (Stanford, 1958) and Nathan Hale, "Origins and Foundations of the Psychoanalytic Movement in America" (University of California at Berkeley, 1965). J. T. Fraser, ed. *The Voices of Time* (New York, 1962), is the best anthology of both the psychology and biology of time. "Time, Instinct, and Freedom" by Henri Bergson, included in Morton White, ed. *The Age of Analysis* (New York, 1955) is essential, and novels of John Dos Passos and William Faulkner's *Sound and the Fury* are good practical examples.

For a background on realism see Robert P. Faulk, "The Rise of Realism, 1871–1891" in Harry Hayden Clark, ed., *Transitions in American Literary History* (Durham, 1953); George J. Becker, ed., *Documents of Modern Literary Realism* (Princeton, 1963); "Realism: An Essay in Definition," *Modern Language Quarterly*, x, June 1949, 184–97; Rene Welleck, "Realism in Literary Scholarship," in *Concepts of Criticism* (New Haven, 1963), pp. 222–55; Everett Carter, *Howells and the Age of Realism* (New York: 1954) and Hamlin Garland, *Crumbling Idols* (Chicago and Cambridge, 1894).

Possibly the best source on realism as a literary method is Harold H. Kolb, *The Illusion of Life, American Realism as a Literary Form* (Charlottesville, 1969). Selected novels of Henry James, Mark Twain, and William Dean Howells are essential literary examples.

The standard sources on pragmatism are Justus Buchler, ed., *The Philosophy of Peirce: Selected Writings* (New York, 1955); William James, *Pragmatism* (New York, 1907); Milton R. Konvitz and Gail Kennedy, eds., *The American Pragmatists*. Max Fisch, *Classic American Philosophers* is an excellent anthology, especially valuable for the introduction. William James' *Psychology* (New York, 1961) and *Varieties of Religious Experience* (New York, 1960) are relevant secondary sources.

The social gospel movement in American life is examined by Charles H. Hopkins in *The Rise of the Social Gospel in American Protestantism 1865–1915* (New Haven, 1967). Some of the best books on revivalism include William G. McLoughlin's *Modern Revivalism* (New York, 1959) and Bernard A. Weisberger's *They Gathered at the River* (Boston, 1958).

II. General Background, 1874–1920

Aaron, Daniel. *Men of Good Hope, A Story of American Progressives.* New York: Oxford University Press, 1961.

Basler, Roy P., Donald H. Mugridge, and Blanche P. McCrum, eds. *A Guide to the Study of the United States of America.* Washington: U.S. Government Printing Office, Library of Congress, 1940, sec. 890.

Beer, Thomas. *The Mauve Decade.* New York: Garden City Publishing Co., Inc., 1926.

Fleming, William. *Arts and Ideas.* New York: Holt, Rinehart and Winston, 1963.

Fraser, J. T., ed. *The Voices of Time.* New York: George Braziller, 1966.

Hofstadter, Richard. *Anti-Intellectualism in American Life.* New York: Vintage Books, 1963.

————. *The Age of Reform.* New York: Vintage Books, 1955.

Mather, Frank Jewett, Jr., Charles Rufus Morey, and William James Henderson. *The American Spirit in Art.* New Haven: Yale University Press, 1927.

May, Henry F. *The End of American Innocence, A Study of the First Years of Our Own Time 1912–1917.* Chicago: Quadrangle Books, 1964.

Miller, Perry, ed. *American Thought Civil War to World War I.* New York: Holt, Rinehart, and Winston, 1965.

Morgan, H. Wayne. *The Gilded Age, A Reappraisal.* Syracuse: Syracuse University Press, 1963.

Newman, James R. *Science and Sensibility,* Vol. II. New York: Simon and Schuster, 1961.

Noble, David W. *The Paradox of Progressive Thought.* Minneapolis: University of Minnesota Press, 1958.

Riley, I. Woodbridge. *American Thought from Puritanism to Pragmatism.* New York: H. Holt & Co., 1915.

Schlissel, Lillian, ed. *The World of Randolph Bourne.* New York: E. P. Dutton & Co., Inc., 1955.

Shattuck, Roger. *The Banquet Years—The Origins of the Avant Garde in France, 1885 to World War I.* New York: Vintage Books, 1968.

Smith, Henry Nash. *Virgin Land, The American West as Symbol and Myth.* New York: Vintage Books, 1950.

White, Morton, ed. *The Age of Analysis, 20th Century.* New York and Toronto: The New American Library, 1955.

————. *Social Thought in America, The Revolt Against Formalism.* Boston: Beacon Press, 1968.

Ziff, Larzer. *The American 1890's.* New York: The Viking Press, 1966.

III. Charles Ives and His Music

Austin, William F. *Music in the Twentieth Century, from Debussy through Stravinsky.* New York: W. W. Norton, 1966.

Boatwright, Howard, ed. *Essays Before a Sonata and Other Writings by Charles Ives.* New York: W. W. Norton & Co., 1961.

Chase, Gilbert, ed. *The American Composer Speaks: A Historical Anthology 1770–1965.* Louisiana: Louisiana State University Press, 1966.

————. *America's Music.* New York: McGraw-Hill Book Company, 1966.

Cooke, Deryck. *The Language of Music.* London: Oxford University Press, 1959.

Cowell, Henry, ed. *American Composers on American Music.* Stanford, California: Stanford University Press, 1933.

————. *New Musical Resources.* New York: Alfred A. Knopf Co., 1930.

Cowell, Henry and Sidney Cowell. *Charles Ives and His Music.* New York: Oxford University Press, 1955.

Epperson, Gordon. *The Musical Symbol, A Study of the Philosophic Theory of Music.* Iowa: Iowa State University Press, 1967.

Ferguson, Donald N. *Music as Metaphor.* Minneapolis: University of Minnesota Press, 1960.

Gurney, Edmund. *The Power of Sound.* London: Smith, Elder & Co., 1880.

Grout, Donald Jay. *A History of Western Music.* New York: W. W. Norton & Co., 1960.

Hansen, Peter S. *An Introduction to Twentieth Century Music.* Boston: Allyn and Bacon, 1967.

Hanslick, Eduard. *The Beautiful in Music.* London: Novello & Co., 1891.

Hitchcock, H. Wiley. *Music in the United States: A Historical Introduction.* Englewood Cliffs, New Jersey: Prentice Hall, Inc., 1969.

Howard, John Tasker. *Our American Music.* New York: Thomas Y. Crowell, 1930.

Hughes, Don Anselm. *The New Oxford History of Music.* London: Oxford University Press, 1954. Vol. II.

Ives, Charles. *Essays Before a Sonata,* ed. by Howard Boatwright. New York: W. W. Norton & Co., Inc., 1964.

de Lerma, Dominique-Rene. *Charles Edward Ives, 1874–1954, A Bibliography of His Music.* Kent, Ohio: Kent State University Press, 1970.

Maisel, Edward M. *Charles T. Griffes.* New York: Alfred A. Knopf, 1943.

Maitland, J. A., ed. *Groves Dictionary of Music and Musicians.* New York: The Macmillan Co., 1907.

Mellers, Wilfred H. *Music in a New Found Land.* New York: Knopf, 1965.

Meyer, Leonard B. *Emotion and Meaning in Music.* Chicago: The University of Chicago Press, 1957.

Nettleton, George H., ed. *The Book of the Yale Pageant.* New Haven: Yale University Press, 1916.

Osterweis, Rollin. *Three Centuries of New Haven.* New Haven: Yale University Press, 1952.

Pierson, George W. *Yale College 1871–1921.* New Haven: Yale University Press, 1952.

Report of the President of *Yale University,* 1894. New Haven: Private Printing, 1894.

Rosenfeld, Paul. *An Hour with American Music.* Philadelphia and London: J. B. Lippincott Co., 1929.

————. *Discoveries of a Music Critic.* New York: Harcourt, Brace and Co., 1936.

————. *Musical Impressions,* ed. Herbert A. Leibowitz. New York: Hill & Wang, 1969.

Rublowsky, John. *Music in America.* New York: Crowell-Collier Press, 1967.

Sablosky, Irving. *American Music.* Chicago and London: The University of Chicago Press, 1969.

Schauffler, Robert Haven, and Sigmund Spaeth. *Music as a Social Force in America and the Science of Practice.* New York: The Caxton Institute, 1972.

Semler, Isabel Parker. *Horatio Parker.* New York: G. Putnam's Sons, 1942.

Sessions, Roger. *Reflections on the Music Life in the United States.* New York: Merlin Press.

Slonimsky, Nicolas. *Music Since 1900.* New York: W. W. Norton & Co., 1937.

Stevenson, Robert. *Protestant Church Music in America.* New York: W. W. Norton & Co., Inc., 1966.

Walker, Alan. *An Anatomy of Musical Criticism.* London: Barrie and Rockliff, 1966.

Westrup, Jack A., and Harrison, F. L. *The New College Encyclopedia of Music.* New York: W. W. Norton & Co., Inc., 1960.

Yates, Peter. *Twentieth Century Music: Its Evolution from the End of the Harmonic Era into the Present Era of Sound.* New York: Pantheon Books, 1967.

Yale University, *Report of the President.* New Haven: Private Annual printing, 1890–1920.

Articles

Bellamann, Henry. "Charles Ives: The Man and His Music," *The Musical Quarterly,* 1933, Vol. 1.

Boatwright, Howard. "Ives' Quarter-Tone Impressions," *Perspectives of New Music,* Vol. 3, No. 2. Spring-Summer, 1965.

Carpenter, Patricia. "The Musical Object," *Current Musicology,* No. 5, 1967.

Carter, Elliott. "Shop Talk by an American Composer," *The Musical Quarterly,* Vol. 46, No. 2, 1960.

————. "The Case of Mr. Ives," *Perspectives of New Music,* Vol. 2, No. 2, 1964.

————. "An American Destiny," *Listen.* IX, November, 1946, 4–7.

————. "Ives Today: His Vision and Challenge." *Modern Music,* XXI, May-June, 1944, 199–202.

————. "The Rhythm Basis of American Music." *Score.* June, 1955.

Cazden, Norman. "Realism in Abstract Music." *Music and Letters,* Vol. XXXVI, 1955. January, p. 38.

Charles, Sydney Robinson. "The Use of Borrowed Material in Ives' Second Symphony." *The Music Review,* VIII, May, 1967, pp. 102–111.

Citkowitz, Israel. "Experiment and Necessity–New York, 1932," *Modern Music,* November, 1933.

Composer's Column (Charles E. Ives). *International Musician,* November, 1949.

Copland, Aaron. "A Businessman Who Wrote Music on Sundays," *Music and Musicians,* 9: 18, November, 1960.

———. "One Hundred and Fourteen Songs," *Modern Music,* XI, January–February, 1934, pp. 59–64.

Cowell, Henry. "American Composers. IX: Charles Ives." *Modern Music,* X, November–December, 1932, pp. 24–32.

———. "Three Native Composers," *The New Freeman,* May 3, 1930.

———. "Charles Ives and His Music," *The Musical Quarterly,* No. 4, 1955.

Downes, Olin. "Charles Ives," *American Composers Alliance,* Vol. 4, No. 1, 1954.

Double Indemnity, Anon. Rev. *Time,* LI, February 23, 1948, pp. 66, 67.

Eger, Joseph. "Ives and the Beatles," *Music Journal,* September, 1968.

Ericson, R. "Charles Ives: *After 55 Years, Still Avant-Garde,*" New York Times, May 24, 1964, p. 113, 18, Sect. 2.

Frankenstein, Alfred. "Ives' Concord Sonata—A Great Day for American Music," *ACA Bulletin,* Special Commemorative Issue, Vol. 10, No. 2, May, 1962.

Grunfeld, Frederic. "Charles Ives: Yankee Rebel," *High Fidelity,* November, 1954.

Gardner, John. "Testing Genius by Analysis," *Composer,* No. 24, Summer, 1967.

Goodman, John. "An Urbanized Thoreau," *The New Leader,* September 23, 1968, pp. 23, 24.

Hall, David. "Charles Ives: An American Original," *HI/FI Stereo Review,* September, 1964.

Harrison, Lou. "On Quotation," *Modern Music,* XXIII, Summer, 1946, pp. 166–169.

Herrmann, Bernard. "Four Symphonies by Charles Ives." *Modern Music,* XXII, May–June 1945, pp. 215–222.

"Insurance Man," Anon. Rev., *Time,* XXXIII, January 30, 1939, pp. 44, 45.

"Charles E. Ives," Anon. Rev., *Life,* October 31, 1949.

Ives, Charles. "Children's Day at the Camp Meeting," *Modern Music,* February 1942.

Ives, Charles E. "The Amount to Carry—Measuring the Prospect," *The Eastern Underwriter,* September 17, 1920, pp. 35–38 (Reprint of Ives' 1912 pamphlet.)

Kelly, June. "American Music Comes of Age," *Music Journal*, September, 1949.

Kirkpatrick, John. "Ives as Revealed in his Marginalia," *The Cornell University Musical Review*, IV, 1961, pp. 14–19.

Klein, Howard, "Ives: A White Heat of Conviction," *The New York Times*, April 16, 1967, p. 26D.

Kolodin, Irving. "A Dream of a Dream—New Ives Hence," *Saturday Review*, May 15, 1965.

Lang, Paul Henry. "Ives in Retrospect." *Saturday Review*, July 1, 1954.

———. "Charles Ives," *Saturday Review*, XXIX, June 1, 1946.

"The Legacy of Charles Ives," *Pan Pipes*, January, 1963, Vol. 55, No. 2.

Lippman, Edward Arthur. "Symbolism in Music," *The Musical Quarterly*, October, 1953, Vol. XXXIX, No. 4.

Maniates, Maria Rika. "Sound, Silence and Time: Towards a Fundamental Ontology of Music," *Current Musicology*, Spring, 1966.

Marshall, Dennis. "Charles Ives' Quotations: Manner or Substance?" *Perspectives of New Music*, Vol. 6, No. 2, Spring-Summer, 1968.

Mellers, W. H. "Music in the Melting Pot," *Scrutiny*, March, 1939.

Moor, Paul. "On Horseback to Heaven: Charles Ives," *Harper's Magazine*, CXCVII, September, 1948, p. 65–73.

———. "Two Titans." *Theatre Arts*, XXIV, ii, February, 1950, pp. 49–51; 94–95.

"Music as a University Course," *The American Monthly Review of Reviews*, Vol. XIV, July 1896, p. 87.

Noske, Fritz R. "Musical Quotation as a Dramatic Device: The Fourth Act of Le Nozze Di Figaro," *The Musical Quarterly*, Vol. LIV, No. 2, April, 1968.

"Notes of the Day," *Monthly Musical Record*, Vol. 85, No. 968, July-August, 1955.

Parker, Horatio, "Addresses, Essays, Lectures, 189?-1919, No. 13, Yale University Library of the School of Music (ma 33-P-A4).

Perkins, Francis D. "In Defense of Critics," *Harper's*, December, 1948.

Pratt, Waldo S. "Music as a University Course," *The American Monthly Review of Reviews*, Vol. XIV, July, 1896, p. 87.

Rosenfeld, Paul. "The Advent of American Music," *Kenyon Review*, Winter, 1939, and Spring, 1939.

———. "A Plea for Improvisation," *Modern Music*, November, 1941.

———. "Charles E. Ives." *The New Republic*, LXXI, July 20, 1932, pp. 262–264.

Sargeant, Winthrop. "Saluting Mr. Ives," *New Yorker*, October 11, 1958.

Sear, H. G. "Charles Ives: Song Writer," *Monthly Musical Record*, February, 1951.

Schonberg, Harold C. "America's Greatest Composer," *Esquire,* December, 1958.

Schrade, Leo. "Charles E. Ives," *Yale Review,* Summer, 1955.

———. "Charles E. Ives: 1874–1954," *The Yale Review,* XLIV, June, 1955, pp. 535, 545.

Slonimsky, Nicholas. "Musical Rebel," *Americas,* September, 1953.

———. "Etude Musical Miscellany," *Etude,* April, 1949.

———. "Bringing Ives Alive," *Saturday Review of Literature,* XXXI, XXXV, August 23, 1948, 45, 49.

———. "Charles Ives—America's Musical Prophet," *Pan Pipes,* 47: 20, January, 1955.

Smith, Max, "Mona," *Musical America,* Vol. XV, No. 20, March 23, 1912, pp. 1–4.

Stambler, Bernard. "Four American Composers," *The Julliard Review* II, Winter, 1955, pp. 7–16.

Stoddard, Hope. "Music in Connecticut," *International Musician,* March, 1951.

Stone, Kurt. "A Postscript on Ives' Fourth," *The Musical Quarterly,* Vol. 52, 1966.

Sun (New York), March 15, 1912, pp. 9, col. 1–3.

Taubman, Howard. "Posterity Catches Up with Charles Ives," *The New York Times Magazine,* October 23, 1949, 15: 34–36. *The Times,* May 16, 1966.

Weerts, Richard. "His Name is Ives," *Musical Journal,* March 5, 1951, 72–74.

"Yankee Music," Anon. Rev., *Time,* LVII, x March 5, 1951, 72–74.

Yates, Peter. "Charles Ives." *Art and Architecture,* LXVII 10, February 1950.

DISSERTATIONS AND THESES

Carlson, Paul B. "An Historical Background and Stylistic Analysis of Three Twentieth Century Compositions for Violin and Piano" (Kansas City, Missouri: The University of Missouri, 1964), unpublished Doctor of Musical Arts Dissertation.

Bryant, Sister Emily Marie, S.P., "The Avant-Garde Character of Charles Ives' Music Exemplified in Various Works" (Los Angeles, California: M.A. Thesis, Mount St. Mary's College).

Kearnes, William Kay, "Horatio Parker 1863–1919: A Study of His Life and Music" (Illinois: University of Illinois unpublished Ph.D. dissertation, 1965).

Layton, Bentley, "The Songs of Charles Ives" (Cambridge, Harvard Bachelor of Arts Thesis, 1963).

Mays, Kenneth Robert. "The Use of Hymn Tunes in the Works of Charles Ives" (Indiana, 1961).

Myers, Betty Dustin. "The Orchestral Music of Charles Ives" (University of Indiana, 1951).

Rosen, Lee Cyril. "The Violin Sonatas of Charles Ives" (University of Illinois, 1965).

Rossiter, Frank. "Charles Ives and American Culture: The Process of Development, 1874–1921" (Princeton University Ph.D. dissertation, July, 1970).

Vinquist, Mary Ann. "The Psalm Settings of Charles Ives" (University of Indiana, 1965).

Ward, Charles M. "The Use of Hymn Tunes as an Expression of Substance and Manner in the Music of Charles Edward Ives 1874–1954" (The University of Texas, M.M. thesis, 1969).

OTHER

Frame, Robert. "Charles Ives: The Tragedy of a Progressive," unpublished undergraduate paper, The University of Minnesota, December 17, 1969.

Ives, Charles. "Foreword" to the Unanswered Question.

Kirkpatrick, John. "A Temporary Mimeographed Catalogue of the Music Manuscripts and related materials of Charles Edward Ives" (New Haven, 1960).

———. "Preface" to Charles E. Ives. *Symphony No. 4* (New York: Associated Music Publishers, Inc., 1965).

Riedel, Johannes, and Robert Oudal. "A Charles Ives' Primer" (University of Minnesota, Minneapolis, 1969). Unpublished introduction to musical idioms in the music.

Rossiter, Frank. Private letter to the author (July 16, 1970).

IV. TRANSCENDENTALISM AND RELIGION

Abrams, M. H. *The Mirror and the Lamp: Romantic Theory and the Critical Tradition* (New York: W. W. Norton, 1958.)

Cabot, James Elliot, ed. *Emerson's Complete Works* (Boston: Houghton Mifflin, & Co., Riverside Edition, 1883–93), Vol. 1.

Cooke, George Willis, ed. *The Early Letters of George William Curtis to John Sullivan Dwight: Brook Farm and Concord* (New York: Harper, 1898).

Cooke, George Willis, *John S. Dwight, Brook Farmer, Editor, and Critic of Music, A Biography* (Boston: Small Maynard, 1898).

Cristy, Arthur. *The Orient in American Transcendentalism* (New York: Octagon Books, Inc., 1963).

Davidson, Audrey. "Transcendental Unity in the Works of Charles Ives," *American Quarterly*, Vol. xxii, No. 1, Spring, 1970, pp. 35–44.

Deussen, Paul. *The Philosophy of the Upanishads*, trans. by A. S. Geden (Edinburgh, 1906).

Dwight, John Sullivan. "The Intellectual Significance of Music." *Dwight's Journal of Music.* XXI, 1862.

———. "The Influence of Music on the Intellectual Powers," *Dwight's Journal of Music,* XXI, 1862.

Emerson, Ralph Waldo. "Lecture on the Times," *The Works of Ralph Waldo Emerson,* Vol. IV (New York: Hearst's International Library Co., 1914).

———. *Miscellanies, Embracing Nature, Addresses and Lectures* (Boston: J. R. Osgood & Co., 1877).

———. *Prose Works of Ralph Waldo Emerson* (Boston: Fields, Osgood & Co., 1870), Vol. I.

———. *The Complete Works of Ralph Waldo Emerson* (Boston and New York: Centenary Edition, 1903–1904), Vol. II.

———. *Basic Selections from Emerson,* ed. Eduard C. Lindeman (New York: Mentor Books, 1954).

Emerson, E. W. *Emerson in Concord.* (Boston and New York: Houghton, Mifflin Co., 1889).

Frothingham, Octavius Brooks. *Transcendentalism in New England* (Boston: American Unitarian Association, 1903).

Fuller, Margaret. "Lives of the Great Composers," *Art, Literature and the Drama,* ed. Arthur B. Fuller (Boston: Brown, Taggard, and Chase, 1860).

———. *Memoirs of Margaret Fuller Ossoli,* II (Boston: Phillips, Sampson, and Co., 1851).

Hall, Manly Palmer. "New England Brahman: Ralph Waldo Emerson," *Horizon,* Vol. I, No. 3, October, 1941.

Harding, Walter, and Clark Bode, eds. *The Correspondence of Henry David Thoreau.* (New York: New York University Press, 1958).

Harding, Walter. *The Days of Henry Thoreau.* (New York: Alfred A. Knopf, 1966).

Harris, Neil. *The Artist in American Society* (New York: George Braziller, 1966).

Hochfield, George, ed. *Selected Writings of the American Transcendentalists* (New York and Toronto: The New American Library, 1966).

Holmes, Oliver Wendell. *Ralph Waldo Emerson* (Boston: Houghton Mifflin, 1885).

Hopkins, Charles H. *The Rise of the Social Gospel in American Protestantism* (New Haven: Yale University Press, 1967).

Hopkins, Vivian C. *Spires of Form, A Study of Emerson's Aesthetic Theory* (Cambridge: Harvard University Press, 1951).

Lovejoy, Arthur Oncken. *The Reason, The Understanding, The Time* (Baltimore: Johns Hopkins Press, 1961).

McLoughlin, William Gerald. *Modern Revivalism* (New York: Ronald Press Co., 1959).

_____. *Billy Sunday Was His Real Name* (Chicago: The University of Chicago Press, 1955).

Matthiessen, F. O. *American Renaissance* (New York: Oxford University Press, 1941).

Miller, Perry, ed. *The Transcendentalists: An Anthology* (Cambridge, Mass.: Harvard University Press, 1967).

_____. "Jonathan Edwards to Emerson," *The New England Quarterly*, Vol. XIII, No. 4, December, 1940.

_____, ed. *Major Writers of America* (New York, San Francisco, Chicago, Atlanta: Harcourt, Brace, & World, Inc., 1962).

Parrington, Vernon L. *Main Currents in American Thought*, Vol. II, "The Romantic Revolution in America" (New York: Harcourt, Brace, & World, Inc., 1939).

Perry, Bliss, ed. *The Heart of Emerson's Journals* (Boston and New York: Houghton Mifflin Co., 1926).

Rider, Daniel E. *The Musical Thought and Activities of the New England Transcendentalists* (University of Minnesota, unpublished Ph.D. dissertation, Fall, 1964).

Riley, I. Woodbridge. *American Thought from Puritanism to Pragmatism* (New York: 1923).

Rusk, Ralph L. *The Life of Ralph Waldo Emerson* (New York: C. Scribner's Sons, 1949).

Santayana, George. *The Genteel Tradition at Bay* (New York: C. Scribner's Sons, 1949).

Simon, Myron, and Thornton H. Parson. *Transcendentalism and Its Legacy* (Ann Arbor: University of Michigan Press, 1966).

Smith, Norris Kelly. *Frank Lloyd Wright* (Englewood Cliffs, New Jersey: Prentice-Hall, Inc., 1966).

Torrey, Bradford, ed. *Journals, Henry David Thoreau* (Boston: Houghton, Mifflin, and Co., 1906).

_____. *The Writings of Henry David Thoreau* (Boston and New York: Houghton, Mifflin, & Co., 1906).

Weisberger, Bernard A. *They Gathered at the River. The Story of the Great Revivalists and Their Impact Upon Religion in America* (Boston, Toronto: Little, Brown and Co., 1958).

Whicher, Stephen E., ed. *Selections from Ralph Waldo Emerson* (Boston: Houghton Mifflin Co., 1957).

V. The Stream of Consciousness

Abbott, Lyman. "The Philosophy of Henri Bergson," *Outlook*, CIII, 1913, pp. 388–391.

Bergson, Henri. *Essai sur les donnees immediates de la conscience* (Paris, 1889), authorized translation by F. L. Pogson as *Time and Free Will: An Essay on the Immediate Data of Consciousness* (London and New York, 1910).

Bergsten, Staffan. *Time and Eternity* (Sweden: Berlingska Boktryckeriet, Lund, 1960).

Brown, Calvin S. *Music and Literature* (Athens, Georgia: University of Georgia Press, 1948).

Brown, James A. C. *Freud and the Post-Freudians* (Baltimore: Md.: Penguin Books, 1967).

Burnham, John C. *Psychoanalysis in American Civilization Before 1918* (Stanford: Stanford University Ph.D. dissertation, 1958).

Dercum, Francis X., "An Evaluation of the Psychogenic Factors in the Etiology of Mental Disease, Including a Review of Psychoanalysis," *Journal American Medical Association* XII, 1914, 753.

Eliot, T. S. *The Waste Land and Other Poems* (New York: Harvest Books, 1962).

Freud, Sigmund. *A General Introduction to Psychoanalysis* (New York: Washington Square Press, Inc., 1962).

————. *The Interpretation of Dreams* (London: The Hogarth Press, 1953).

Hale, Nathan George. *The Origins and Foundation of the Psychoanalytic Movement in America, 1909–1914* (California: University of California, Berkeley Ph.D. dissertation, 1965).

Hall, Calvin S. *A Primer of Freudian Psychology* (New York: The New American Library, 1963).

Hall, Trevor H. *The Strange Case of Edmund Gurney* (London: W.C.2: Gerald Duckworth & Co., LTD., 1964).

Hughes, H. Stuart. *Consciousness and Society* (New York: Vintage Books, 1958).

Humphrey, Robert. *The Stream of Consciousness in the Modern Novel* (Berkeley and Los Angeles: University of California Press, 1955).

James, William. *The Principles of Psychology* (New York: Henry Holt, 1890), I.

————. *Psychology*, edited by Gordon Allport (New York: Harper and Row, 1961).

————. *The Varieties of Religious Experience* (New York: Mentor Book of the New American Library, 1958).

Jones, Genesius. *Approach to the Purpose* (London: Hodder and Stoughton, 1964).

Jung, Carl. *The Psychology of Dementia Praecox* (New York: Journal of Nervous and Mental Disease Publishing Co., 1908).

————. *Modern Man in Search of a Soul.* New York: Random House, 1933.

Lovejoy, Arthur O. "The Metaphysician of the Life Force," *The Nation,* LXXXIX, 1909, 298–301.

Martin, P. W. *Experiment in Depth. A Study of the Work of Jung, Eliot, and Toynbee* (London, 1955).

Matthiessen, F. O. *The Achievements of T. S. Eliot* (Boston and New York: Houghton Mifflin Co., 1935).

Maude, John Edward. "The Unconscious in Education," *Education,* II, 1882, 394–409; 459–476.

Murphy, Gardner, and Robert O. Ballou. *William James on Psychical Research* (New York: The Viking Press, 1960).

Prince, Morton. *The Nature of Mind and Human Automatism* (Philadelphia: J. B. Lippincott, 1885).

————. "The Educational Treatment of Neurasthenia," *Boston Medical and Surgical Journal,* CXXXIX, 1898, p. 335.

————. "The Psychological Principles and Field of Psychotherapy," *Psychotherapeutics* (Boston: Richard C. Badger, 1909).

Proust, Marcel. *Remembrance of Things Past* (New York: Random House, 1934).

Rieff, Philip. *Freud: The Mind of the Moralist* (Garden City, New York: Doubleday & Co., Inc., 1961).

Runes, D. D., ed. *The Dictionary of Philosophy* (New York: The Philosophical Library, 1942).

Smith, Ely Jellife. "The Review of Carl Jung, The Psychology of the Unconscious," *The Journal of Nervous and Mental Disease,* XLIV, 1916, pp. 382–384.

VI. Realism

Becker, George J. "Realism: An Essay in Definition," *Modern Language Quarterly,* X, June, 1949, 184–97.

————. *Documents of Modern Literary Realism* (Princeton, New Jersey: Princeton University Press, 1967).

Bellamy, Edward. *Looking Backward* (New York: The New American Library, 1964).

Bierce, Ambrose. *The Devil's Dictionary* (New York: Hill and Wang, 1957).

Brown, Calvin S. *The Reader's Companion to World Literature* (New York: The New American Library, 1959).

Carter, Everett. *Howells and the Age of Realism* (New York and Connecticut: Shoe String Press, 1954).

Chase, Richard. *The American Novel and Its Tradition* (Garden City, New York: Doubleday & Co., 1957).

Chiari, Joseph. *Realism and Imagination* (London: Barrie and Rockliff, 1960).

Clark, Harry Hayden, ed. *Transitions in American Literary History* (New York: Octagon Books, Inc., 1967).

Cummings, E. E. *Six Non-Lectures* (Cambridge: Harvard University Press, 1953).

Cunliffe, Marcus. *The Literature of the United States* (Baltimore, Maryland: Penguin Books, 1967).

DeForest, John William. *Miss Ravenal's Conversion from Secession to Loyalty* (New York: Holt, Rinehart and Winston, 1965).

Dreiser, Theodore. *Sister Carrie* (New York: The New American Library, 1962).

Edel, Leon. *Henry James, A Collection of Critical Essays* (Englewood Cliffs, New Jersey: Prentice-Hall, Inc., 1963).

———. *The Selected Letters of Henry James* (New York: Farrar, Straus, and Cudahy, 1955).

Flaubert, Gustave. "On Realism," *Documents of Modern Realism* (New Jersey: Princeton University Press, 1967).

Forbes, Allyn B. "The Literary Quest for Utopia, 1880–1900," *Social Forces,* Vol. VI, No. 2, December, 1927.

Garland, Hamlin. *Crumbling Idols* (Gainesville, Florida: Scholars' Facsimiles and Reprints, 1952).

Grattan, C. Hartley. *The Three Jameses* (New York: New York University Press, 1962).

Hornstein, G. D., Sterling Brown Percy. eds. *The Reader's Companion to World Literature* (New York: Mentor Books, 1956).

James, Henry, *The American* (New York: The New American Library, 1963).

Kazin, Alfred. *On Native Grounds* (New York: Reynal and Hitchcock, 1942).

Knight, Grant C. *The Critical Period in American Literature* (Chapel Hill: The University of North Carolina Press, 1951).

Kolb, Harold H. *The Illusion of Life. American Realism as a Literary Form* (Charlottesville: The University Press of Virginia, 1969).

Lowes, John Livingston. *Convention and Revolt in Poetry* (Boston and New York: Houghton Mifflin Co., 1919).

Martin, Jay. *Harvests of Change, American Literature 1865–1914* (Englewood Cliffs, New Jersey: Prentice-Hall, Inc., 1967).

McMurry, Donald le Crone. *Coxey's Army: A Study of the Industrial Army Movement of 1894* (Boston: Little Brown, & Co., 1929).

Miller, Perry, ed. *Major Writers of America, II* (New York, San Francisco, Chicago, Atlanta: Harcourt, Brace, & World, Inc., 1962).

Richardson, Lyon N., ed. *Henry James, Representative Selections* (Urbana and London: University of Illinois Press, 1966).

Thorp, Willard, ed. *Great Short Works of American Realism* (New York: Harper & Row, 1968).

Twain, Mark. *Adventures of Huckleberry Finn* (Boston: Houghton, Mifflin Company, 1958).

Walcutt, Charles Child. *American Literary Naturalism, A Divided Stream* (Minneapolis: University of Minnesota Press, 1956).

Wellek, Rene. *Concepts of Criticism* (New Haven and London: Yale University Press, 1963).

Wilson, Colin. *The Strength to Dream. Literature and the Imagination* (London: Victor Gollancz Ltd., 1962).

VII. PRAGMATISM

Allen, Gay Wilson. *William James, A Biography* (New York: The Viking Press, 1967).

DeBary, William Theodore, ed. *Introduction to Oriental Civilizations, Sources of Indian Tradition* (New York: Columbia University Press, 1960).

Buchler, Justus, ed. *The Philosophy of Peirce: Selected Writings* (New York: Dover Publications, 1955).

Chisolm, Lawrence W. *Fenollosa: The Far East and American Culture* (New Haven and London: Yale University Press, 1963).

Conkin, Paul K. *Puritans and Pragmatists* (New York and Toronto: Dodd, Mead, and Co., 1968).

Crunden, Robert M. *A Hero in Spite of Himself: Brand Whitlock in Art, Politics, and War* (New York: Knopf, 1969).

Fenollosa, Ernest. *The Chinese Written Character as a Medium for Poetry* (New York: Arrow Editions, 1936).

Fisch, Max. *Classic American Philosophers* (New York: Meredith Corporation, 1951).

––––––. "Justice Holmes, the Prediction Theory of Law, and Pragmatism," *Journal of Philosophy* 39: 85–97, February 12, 1942.

Grattan, Clinton Hartley. *The Three Jameses* (New York: New York University Press, The Gotham Library, 1962).

Gulick, Sidney Lewis. *The East and the West. A Study of Their Psychic and Cultural Characteristics* (Rutland, Vermont and Tokyo, Japan: Charles E. Tuttle, Co., 1963).

Hartshorne, Charles and Paul Weiss, eds. *The Collected Papers of Charles Sanders Peirce* (Cambridge, Mass.: Harvard University Press, 1931–1935), Vol. 1–6.

Hofstadter, Richard. *Social Darwinism in American Thought* (Boston: Beacon Press, 1966).

The Impact of Darwinian Thought on American Life and Culture. Papers read at the Fourth Annual Meeting of the American Studies Association of Texas. Austin: The University of Texas, 1959.

James, William. *Essays in Pragmatism,* ed. by Alburey Castell (New York: Hafner Publishing Co., 1965).

––––––. *The Varieties of Religious Experience* (New York: Mentor Books, 1958).

––––––. "The Final Impressions of a Psychical Researcher," *The American Magazine,* October, 1909.

_____ . *Pragmatism: A New Name for Some Old Ways of Thinking* (New York: Longmans, Green & Co., 1959).

_____ . *Psychology,* Gordon Allport, ed. (New York: Harper and Row, 1961).

_____ . *Human Immortality: Two Supposed Objections to the Doctrine* (Boston and New York: Houghton, Mifflin, & Co., 1898).

James, Henry, ed. *The Letters of William James* (Boston: Atlantic Monthly Press, 1920), Vol. I.

Keyserling, Count Hermann. *Diary* I, trans. by J. Holroyd Reece (London: J. Cape Ltd., 1925).

Konvitz, Milton R. and Gail Kennedy, eds. *The American Pragmatists* (New York: Meridian Books, Inc., 1960).

Langer, Suzanne K. *Philosophical Sketches* (New York: Mentor Press, 1964).

Matthiessen, F. O. *The James Family* (New York: Alfred A. Knopf, 1961).

Moore, Edward C. *American Pragmatism: Peirce, James, and Dewey* (New York: Columbia University Press, 1961).

Murphy, Gardner, and Robert O. Ballou, eds. *William James on Psychical Research* (New York: The Viking Press, 1960).

Perry, Ralph Barton. *The Thought and Character of William James* (New York: George Braziller, 1954).

Persons, Stow, ed. *Evolutionary Thought in America* (New York: George Braziller, Inc., 1950).

_____ . "Darwinism and American Culture," *The Impact of Darwinian Thought on American Life and Culture* (Austin: The University of Texas, 1959).

Pratt, James B. *What is Pragmatism?* (New York: Macmillan Co., 1909).

Rorty, Amelie, ed. *Pragmatic Philosophy, an Anthology* (New York: Doubleday & Co., Inc., 1966).

Santayana, George. *Scepticism and Animal Faith* (New York: Charles Scribner's Sons, 1929).

_____ . "The Genteel Tradition in American Philosophy," in Myron Simon and Thornton H. Parsons, *Transcendentalism and Its Legacy* (Ann Arbor: University of Michigan Press, 1966).

_____ . *Persons and Places, The Background of My Life* (New York: Charles Scribner's Sons, 1944).

Stevenson, Elizabeth. *Lafacadio Hearn* (New York: The Macmillan Co., 1961).

NOTES

1. Morton White, ed., *The Age of Analysis, Twentieth Century Philosophers* (New York and Toronto: The New American Library, 1955), p. 67.

CHAPTER I

1. Henry Cowell and Sidney Cowell, *Charles Ives and His Music* (London, Oxford, New York: Oxford University Press, 1955), p. 37.

2. Cowell, *Charles Ives,* p. 22.

3. The Alumni Records Office has a folder for Ives containing about 50 items—1894-date-extracts from newspaper and magazine articles, alumni communications, blanks for the Alumni Register filled out, and so on.

4. George Wilson Pierson, *Yale College 1871-1921* (New Haven: Yale University Press, 1952), p. 5.

5. *Ibid.,* p. 7.

6. *Ibid.,* p. 8.

7. *Ibid.,* p. 10.

8. *Ibid.,* p. 19.

9. David Stanley Smith, *Gustave J. Stoeckel, Yale Pioneer in Music* (New Haven: Yale University Press, 1939), pp. 4, 6.

10. *Report of the President of Yale University, 1894* (New Haven: Private Printing, 1894), 4.

11. Horatio William Parker, *Lectures on the History of Music,* No. 1, p. 4.

12. William Kay Kearnes, *Horatio Parker 1863-1919: A Study of His Life and Music* (Illinois: University of Illinois unpublished Ph.D. dissertation, 1965), p. 118. I am much indebted to Kearnes work for insight and analysis of this composer.

13. Horatio William Parker, "Music at Yale," *The Book of the Yale Pageant,* ed. by George H. Nettleton (New Haven: Yale University Press, 1916), p. 228.

14. Waldo S. Pratt, "Music as a University Course," *The American Monthly Review of Reviews,* Vol. xɪv, July 1896, p. 87.

15. Kearnes, *Horatio Parker,* p. 124.

16. Psychologists have proved that people often adopt the same qualities in others that make them miserable personally. This is apparently a means of psychic defense; i.e., to avoid being eaten by a dragon, become a dragon yourself. It is my opinion that the humorous and highly original mind of Charles Ives—a mind exactly opposite to that of Parker—could neither adopt the fear authoritarianism of Parker's domination and all it meant, nor reject it. Consequently, his only course was to take a job in another field and keep his music private and protected. That he perpetually drew on his past and developed many of Parker's ideas is a tribute to Parker's intelligence and influence. That he would choose not to work in the music world may show the wounding of a deeply sensitive mind and the disadvantages of his education, as well as underline his inability to "succeed" as a composer.

17. John Tasker Howard, *Our American Music* (New York: Thomas Y. Crowell, 1930), 376.

18. Kearnes, *Horatio Parker,* p. 16.

19. Actually, Schubert was eighteen when he composed this work and the usual translation of the Kerlkönig is Erlking.

20. Isabel Parker Semler, *Horatio Parker* (New York: G. Putnam's Sons, 1942), p. 302.

21. Cf. Charles M. Ward, *The Use of Hymn Tunes As An Expression of "Substance and Manner" in the Music of Charles Edward Ives 1874–1954"* (The University of Texas, unpublished Master's thesis, 1969).

22. Semler, *Horatio Parker,* p. 163.

23. *Ibid.,* pp. 74, 75.

24. Max Smith, on *Mona, Musical America,* Vol. xv, No. 20 (March 23, 1912), pp. 1-4.

25. *Sun* (New York), March 15, 1912, p. 9, col. 1-3, also quoted in Kearnes.

26. Kearnes, *Horatio Parker,* p. 684.

27. Horatio Parker, "Addresses, Essays, Lectures," 189?-1919, No. 13. Yale University Library of the School of Music (MA 33-P-A4).

28. George W. Chadwick, *Harmony, A Course of Study* (Boston: B. F. Wood Music Co., 1897).

29. Cowell, *Charles Ives,* pp. 33, 34.

30. Kearnes, *Horatio Parker,* p. 8.

31. *Ibid.,* p. 5.

32. Cowell, *Charles Ives,* p. 33.

33. *Ibid.,* p. 36.

34. Establishing dates for Ives' music is difficult because Ives often dated a piece by its last revision, no matter how long this might be after the composition.

35. Quoted in John Kirkpatrick, *The Memos of Charles Ives,* to be published by W. W. Norton, 1971, ms. p. 101.

36. From material in The Ives Collection, Yale University Music Library, New Haven, Connecticut.

37. Charles Ives, *Essays Before a Sonata and Other Writings*, Howard Boatwright, ed., (New York: W. W. Norton & Co., Inc., 1964), p. 119.

38. Quoted in John Kirkpatrick, "A Temporary Mimeographed Catalogue of The Music Manuscripts and Related Materials of Charles Edward Ives" (New Haven, 1960), p. iv.

39. Cowell, *Charles Ives*, p. 75.

40. David W. Noble, "The Paradox of Progressive Thought," *The American Experience*, ed. Hennig Cohen (Boston: Houghton Mifflin, 1968), pp. 184–195; see also David W. Noble, *The Paradox of Progressive Thought* (Minneapolis: University of Minnesota, 1958).

41. Noble, *The Paradox*, p. 185.

42. Ives, *Essays*, p. 130.

43. Charles Ives died Wednesday morning, May 19, 1954 around 2:30 A.M. at the Roosevelt Hospital, New York. John Kirkpatrick, in a letter to Carl and Charlotte Ruggles (Friday, May 21, 1954) said that Ives had been operated on for a double hernia and that the operation had been a success, but that Ives had had something like a stroke.

CHAPTER 2

1. Arthur Christy, *The Orient in American Transcendentalism* (New York: Octagon Books, Inc., 1963), p. 3.

2. Oliver Wendell Holmes, *Ralph Waldo Emerson* (Boston: Houghton Mifflin, 1885), p. 287.

3. Quoted in Ralph L. Rusk, *The Life of Ralph Waldo Emerson* (New York: C. Scribner's Sons, 1949), p. 313.

4. Perry Miller, ed. "Ralph Waldo Emerson," *Major Writers of America*, I (New York, San Francisco, Chicago, Atlanta: Harcourt, Brace & World, Inc., 1962), p. 481.

5. Wilfred H. Mellers, *Music in a New Found Land* (New York: Knopf, 1965), pp. 38–64. Gilbert Chase, *America's Music* (New York: McGraw-Hill Book Company), p. 406.

6. Myron Simon and Thornton H. Parsons, ed., *Transcendentalism and Its Legacy* (Ann Arbor: The University of Michigan Press, 1966), p. 59. See also E. W. Emerson, *Emerson in Concord* (Boston and New York: Houghton, Mifflin Co., 1889). James E. Cabot, *A Memoir of Ralph Waldo Emerson* (Boston and New York: Houghton, Mifflin, & Co., 1887).

7. Frank Rossiter, *Charles Ives and American Culture: The Process of Development, 1874–1921* (Princeton: Princeton University, dissertation for Ph.D., July, 1970).

8. Frank Rossiter, letter to the author, August 1970.

9. George Santayana, *The Genteel Tradition at Bay* (New York: C. Scribner's Sons, 1931), p. 36.

10. Walter Harding, *The Days of Henry Thoreau* (New York: Alfred A. Knopf, 1966), pp. 265 and 362. Some of Thoreau's favorite songs were Mrs. Heman's "Pilgrim Fathers", Moore's "Evening Bells" and "Canadian Boat Song," Wolfe's "Burial of Sir John Moore" and the song "Tom Bowline."

11. Charles Ives, *Essays Before a Sonata,* edited by Howard Boatwright (New York: W. W. Norton & Co., 1962).

12. Henry D. Thoreau, *Early Spring in Massachusetts and Summer, From the Journal* (Boston & New York: Houghton Mifflin Co., 1929) p. 86.

13. F. B. Sanborn, *The Life of Henry David Thoreau* (Boston and New York: Houghton Mifflin Co., 1917. Republished by Gale Research Co., Detroit, 1968) p. 266.

14. Harrison Gray Otis Blake of Worcester, Mass. was in the Harvard class of 1835, two years ahead of Thoreau's class. He was also a member of the Harvard Divinity School class that had invited Emerson to speak at their graduation, the occasion for the "Divinity School Address." Blake later became a teacher. Thoreau wrote about fifty letters to him.

15. *The Correspondence of Henry David Thoreau,* ed. Walter Harding and Carl Bode (New York: New York University Press, 1958), p. 331. Quoted in Daniel E. Rider, *The Musical Thought and Activities of the New England Transcendentalists* (University of Minnesota, unpublished Ph.D. dissertation, Fall, 1964) p. 272. I am much indebted to Rider for leading me to several primary sources I might otherwise have missed.

16. Walter Harding, *A Thoreau Handbook* (New York: New York University Press, 1959) p. 156.

17. Thoreau, *Journals,* IV (Boston: Houghton Mifflin and Co., 1906), p. 214, recently reprinted (New York: Dover, 1963). Also quoted in Harding, *Days,* p. 296.

18. Vivian C. Hopkins, *Spires of Form, A Study of Emerson's Aesthetic Theory* (Cambridge: Harvard University Press, 1951) pp. 191–193. Hopkins points out Emerson's great interest in music's effect on the mind and the imagination.

19. Margaret Fuller, *Memoirs,* quoted in Perry Miller, *The Transcendentalists, An Anthology* (Cambridge, Mass: Harvard University Press, 1967) p. 337.

20. Rider, *The Musical Thought,* p. 66.

21. John Sullivan Dwight, "The Influence of Music on the Intellectual Powers," *Dwight's Journal of Music* (XXI, 1862), p. 91. Quoted in Rider, *The Musical Thought,* p. 204.

22. Rider, *The Musical Thought,* pp. 211, 212.

23. Perry Miller, ed. *The Transcendentalists: An Anthology* (Cambridge, Mass.: Harvard University Press, 1967) p. 412. Quoted from John Sullivan Dwight's paper, "Music," originally written for Elizabeth Peabody's "Aesthetic Papers," pp. 25–36.

24. *Ibid.,* p. 411.

25. Edward Cary, *George William Curtis,* (New York: Greenwood Press, Publishers, 1969) p. 73.

26. Rider, *The Musical Thought,* p. 26.

27. Many viewed this kind of thinking as a throwback to the messy emotionalism and dangerous mysticism that "liberal Christianity" had striven for a century to exorcise. Cf., Perry Miller, *The Transcendentalists, An Anthology,* p. 11.

28. Rider, *The Musical Thought,* p. 40.

29. Ralph Waldo Emerson, "Lectures on the Times," *The Works of Ralph Waldo Emerson,* Vol. IV (New York: Hearst's International Library Co., 1914), p. 271.

30. Wilfrid Mellers, *Music in a New Found Land,* p. 45.

31. Cf. Sigmund Freud, *The Interpretation of Dreams* (London: The Hogarth Press, 1953), SE V, 372.

32. Charles Ives, *Essays,* p. 7.

33. Bentley Layton, *An Introduction to the 114 Songs of Charles Ives* (Cambridge: Harvard University B.A. thesis, 1963), p. 93.

34. M. H. Abrams, *The Mirror and the Lamp: Romantic Theory and the Critical Tradition* (New York: W. W. Norton, 1958), passim.

35. Charles Ives, preface to *Second Pianoforte Sonata,* "Concord, Mass., 1840–1860" (Redding, Conn.: The Composer, 1920).

36. Donald Jay Grout, *A History of Western Music* (New York: W. W. Norton and Co., Inc., 1960), p. 263.

37. Charles Ives, *Essays,* p. 98.

38. *Ibid.,* p. 99.

39. Willi Apel, *Harvard Dictionary of Music,* (Cambridge, Massachusetts, Harvard University Press, 1962), pp. 277–279.

40. Charles Ives, *Essays,* p. 99.

41. Apel, *Harvard Dictionary,* p. 279.

42. Neil Harris, *The Artist in American Society* (New York: George Braziller, 1966), p. 178.

43. Ralph Waldo Emerson, *The Complete Works of Ralph Waldo Emerson,* Centenary Edition (Boston and New York: 1903–1904), II, p. 374.

44. Bradford Torrey, ed., *The Writings of Henry David Thoreau* (Boston and New York: Houghton, Mifflin, & Co., 1906), p. 52.

45. F. O. Matthiessen, *American Renaissance* (New York: Oxford University Press, 1941), p. 80.

46. Charles Ives, "Some Quarter Tone Impressions," in *Essays,* p. 119.

47. Ralph Waldo Emerson, "The American Scholar," *Major Writers of America,* Perry Miller, ed. (New York, Chicago, San Francisco, Atlanta: Harcourt, Brace, & World), p. 508.

48. Ralph Waldo Emerson, *Journal,* June 24, 1840. The *Heart of Emerson's Journals,* edited by Bliss Perry (Boston and New York: Houghton Mifflin Co., 1926), p. 154.

49. Simon and Parsons, *Transcendentalism,* pp. 9, 10.

50. Eduard C. Lindeman, ed., *Basic Selections from Emerson* (New York: Mentor Books, 1954), p. 215.

CHAPTER 3

1. Morton Prince, *The Nature of Mind and Human Automatism* (Philadelphia: J. B. Lippincott, 1885), p. 153.

2. John Edward Maude, "The Unconscious in Education," *Education*, II (1882), 394-409, 459-476.

3. John C. Burnham, *Psychoanalysis in American Civilization Before 1918* (Stanford University, unpublished Ph.D. dissertation, 1958), p. 354. I am much indebted to Burnham's work for ideas and leads to other sources I might have otherwise missed.

4. Morton Prince, "The Educational Treatment of Neurasthenia," *Boston Medical and Surgical Journal*, CXXXIX (1898), p. 335. Quoted in Hale, *The Origins*, p. 182.

5. Morton Prince, "The Psychological Principles and Field of Psychotherapy," *Psychotherapeutics* (Boston: Richard G. Badger, 1909), pp. 14-16. Quoted in Hale, *The Origins*, p. 180.

6. Frances X. Dercum, "An Evaluation of the Psychogenic Factors in the Etiology of Mental Disease, Including a Review of Psychoanalysis, *Journal of the American Medical Association*, XII, 1914, p. 753. Quoted in Hale, *The Origins*, p. 314.

7. Arthur O. Lovejoy, "The Metaphysician of the Life Force," *The Nation*, LXXXIX (1909), pp. 298-301. Cf. Hale, *The Origins*, p. 44.

8. Ely Jellife Smith, "Review of Carl Jung, The Psychology of the Unconscious," *The Journal of Nervous and Mental Disease*, XLIV, 1916, pp. 382-384. See also, Lyman Abbott, "The Philosophy of Henri Bergson," *Outlook*, CIII, (1913), pp. 388-391. Quoted in Hale, *The Origins*, p. 44.

9. Carl Jung, *The Psychology of Dementia Praecox* (New York: Journal of Nervous and Mental Disease Publishing Co., 1909), pp. 36, 35-38. Cf. Hale, *The Origins*, p. 224.

10. George Nathan Hale, *The Origins and Foundation of the Psychoanalytic Movement in America, 1909-1914* (University of California, Berkeley, 1965), unpublished Ph.D. dissertation, p. 175. I am indebted to Hale's work for ideas and leads to many sources in the psychoanalytic movement.

11. *Ibid.*, p. 176.

12. William James, *The Principles of Psychology* (New York: Henry Holt, 1890), I, p. 239.

13. D. D. Runes, ed., *The Dictionary of Philosophy* (New York: The Philosophical Library, 1942). Also quoted in Humphrey, p. 2.

14. Robert Humphrey, *Stream of Consciousness in the Modern Novel* (Berkeley and Los Angeles: University of California Press, 1955), p. 7.

15. Quoted in John Kirkpatrick, "Preface," *The Fourth Symphony* (New York: Associated Music Publishers).

16. *Ibid.*, pp. i–x.

17. Morton White, ed., *The Age of Analysis, Twentieth Century Philosophers* (New York and Toronto: The New American Library, 1955), p. 68.

18. Charles Ives, "Notes on Fourth Violin Sonata," *Violin and Piano Sonata No. 4*, "Children's Day at the Camp Meeting" (New York: Arrow Music Press, 1942).

19. Acculturation does seem to enter in, since for a suspension of mental content the person must know the task to begin with.

20. Charles Ives, Foreword, *The Unanswered Question,* Southern Music Company, Inc., copyright 1953.

21. Cowell, *Charles Ives,* p. 72.

22. Humphrey, *Stream,* p. 73.

23. Ives, *Essays,* p. 7.

24. Dom Anselm Hughes, ed., *The New Oxford History of Music,* "Early Medieval Music Up to 1300," Vol. II (London: Oxford University Press, 1954), p. 251.

25. John Kirkpatrick, "Preface," *The Fourth Symphony* (New York: Associated Music Publishers).

26. Ives, *Essays,* p. 22.

27. *Ibid.,* p. 24.

CHAPTER 4

1. Charles Child Walcutt, *American Literary Naturalism, A Divided Stream* (Minneapolis: University of Minnesota Press, 1956), pp. vii, 10, 11.

2. Stephen E. Whicher, ed., *Selections from Ralph Waldo Emerson* (Boston: Houghton Mifflin Co., 1957), p. 32.

3. George J. Becker, *Documents of Modern Literary Realism* (Princeton, New Jersey: Princeton University Press, 1967), p. 4.

4. Ambrose Bierce, *The Devil's Dictionary* (New York: Hill & Wang, 1957), p. 152.

5. Alfred Kazin, *On Native Grounds* (New York: Reynal and Hitchcock, 1942), p. 207.

6. Charles Ives, "Some Quarter Tone Impressions," *Essays Before a Sonata,* ed. Howard Boatwright (New York: W. W. Norton & Co., Inc., 1964), p. 108.

7. Charles Ives, *Essays,* p. 88.

8. *Ibid.,* p. 24.

9. *Ibid.,* p. 84.

10. *Ibid.*

11. Edward Arthur Lippman, "Symbolism in Music," *The Musical Quarterly,* October 1953, Vol. XXXIX, No. 4, p. 555.

12. Quote included in John Kirkpatrick, ed., *The Memos of Charles Ives,* to be published by W. W. Norton in 1971.

13. Dagobert D. Runes, *The Dictionary of Philosophy* (New York: Philosophical Library, 1942), p. 264. Realism also is used to signify the belief that physical objects exist independently of experience. See J. O. Urmson, ed., *The Concise Encyclopedia of Western Philosophy and Philosophers* (New York: Hawthorn Books, Inc., 1960).

14. Cf. Rene' Welleck, *Concepts of Criticism* (New Haven and London: Yale University Press, 1963), p. 237.

15. Quote included in John Kirkpatrick, ed., *The Memos of Charles Ives,* to be published by W. W. Norton in 1971.

16. Charles Ives, *Essays*, pp. 80, 81.

17. Eduard C. Lindeman, ed., "Self Reliance," *Basic Selections from Emerson* (New York: Mentor Books, 1954), passim.

18. George J. Becker, "Realism: An Essay in Definition," *Modern Language Quarterly* x, June, 1949, pp. 184–197.

19. Harold H. Kolb, *The Illusion of Life, American Realism as a Literary Form* (Charlottesville: The University Press of Virginia, 1969), p. 34.

20. Harold Kolb, *The Illusion of Life*, p. 99.

21. Henry James, *The Bostonians* (London and New York: Macmillan and Co., 1886), p. 449.

22. Henry James, *The American* (New York: The New American Library, 1963), pp. 324, 325.

23. Johannes Riedel and Robert Oudal, "A Charles Ives' Primer" (University of Minnesota, Minneapolis, 1969), unpublished.

24. Charles Ives, *Essays*, p. 92.

25. *Ibid.*, p. 92.

26. Henry and Sydney Cowell, *Charles Ives*, p. 148.

27. Cowell, *Charles Ives*, p. 157.

28. Cowell, *Charles Ives*, p. 106.

29. Harold Kolb, *The Illusion of Life*, pp. 49, 50.

30. Charles Ives, "The Greatest Man," quoted in R. S. Perry's unpublished Ph.D. dissertation "Charles Ives and American Culture" (Texas: The University of Texas, 1971), p. 150.

31. E. E. Cummings, *Six Non-Lectures* (Cambridge: Harvard University Press, 1953), pp. 6, 7.

32. Cowell, *Charles Ives*, p. 79.

CHAPTER 5

1. Bernard A. Weisberger, *They Gathered at the River* (Boston, Toronto: Little, Brown and Co., 1958), p. 19.

2. Lowell Mason, "Watchman Tell Us of the Night," *The Presbyterian Hymnal* (Richmond, Virginia: Presbyterian Committee of Publication, 1928), No. 393.

3. William G. McLoughlin, Jr., *Modern Revivalism, Charles Grandison Finney to Billy Graham* (New York: Ronald Press Co., 1959), p. 7.

4. Ives, deeply impressed by revivals of his youth, thought in his later years that the camp-meetings were becoming "easy-bodied and commercialized." He thought such revivalists as Amy McPherson were just a form of "easy entertainment and silk cushions—far different from the days of 'stone-fielders.' " See John Kirkpatrick's *Memos of Charles Ives*. (p. 99 of ms.)

5. Cowell, *Charles Ives*, p. 24. I am also indebted to Martha Doty, a graduate student friend at The University of Texas, for initially calling my attention to revivalism in Ives' music.

6. Quoted in John Livingston Lowes, *Convention and Revolt in Poetry* (Boston and New York: Houghton Mifflin Co., 1919), p. 175.

7. Bernard A. Weisberger, *They Gathered at the River*, Boston, Toronto: Little, Brown and Company, 1958), pp. 249, 250.

8. William G. McLoughlin, *Billy Sunday Was His Real Name* (Chicago: The University of Chicago Press, 1955), p. 171.

9. *Ibid.*, p. 26.

10. Henry F. May, *The End of American Innocence* (Chicago: Quadrangle Books, 1964), p. 127.

11. For this musical example, see Chapter 2, p. 39.

12. Weisberger, *They Gathered at the River*, p. 252.

13. Charles H. Hopkins, *The Rise of the Social Gospel in American Protestantism 1865-1915* (New Haven: Yale University Press, 1965), passim and p. 318-327.

14. See Mary Ann Vinquist, "The Psalm Settings of Charles Ives" (University of Indiana, 1965), unpublished Master of Arts thesis.

15. Charles Ives, *Essays*, p. 36.

16. Allyn B. Forbes, "The Literary Quest for Utopia, 1880-1900," *Social Forces*, Vol. vi, No. 2, December, 1927.

17. Jay Martin, *Harvests of Change* (Englewood Cliffs, N.J.: Prentice-Hall, Inc., 1967), p. 213.

18. *Ibid.*, pp. 202-226.

19. Charles Ives, *Nov. 2, 1920* (Bryn Mawr, Pennsylvania. New Music Editions, Theodore Presser Company, 1921). Originally included in Ives' *114 Songs* (privately printed).

20. Cf. Gordon Epperson, "The Symbolist Poets and Their Influence," *The Musical Symbol, A Study of the Philosophic Theory of Music* (Iowa: Iowa State University Press, 1967), Chapter 8, pp. 189-216.

21. Edward Arthur Lippman, "Symbolism in Music," *The Musical Quarterly*, October, 1953, Vol. xxxix, No. 4.

22. Cowell, *Charles Ives*, p. 202.

23. *Ibid.*, p. 202.

24. Daniel Aaron, *Men of Good Hope, A Story of American Progressives* (New York: Oxford University Press, 1961), p. 246.

25. *Ibid.*, p. 282.

26. Ives, *Essays*, p. 29.

27. *Ibid.*, p. 28.

28. *Ibid.*, p. 35.

29. Cowell, *Charles Ives,* p. 93.

30. Ives, *Essays,* p. 62.

31. Cf. Henry May, *The End,* pp. 125, 126.

CHAPTER 6

1. Harold H. Kolb, *The Illusion of Life, American Realism as a Literary Form* (Charlottesville: The University Press of Virginia, 1969), p. 94.

2. Mark Twain, *Adventures of Huckleberry Finn* (Boston: Houghton Mifflin Co., 1958), p. 206.

3. Stow Persons, "Darwinism and American Culture," *The Impact of Darwinian Thought on American Life and Culture* (Austin: The University of Texas, 1959), p. 7.

4. Richard Hofstadter, *Social Darwinism in American Thought* (Boston: Beacon Press, 1966), pp. 124, 125.

5. Stow Persons, "Darwinism," p. 8.

6. Stow Persons, ed., *Evolutionary Thought in America* (New York: George Braziller, Inc., 1956), pp. 191–195. The transformation of the Darwinian hypothesis into a creed of social reform is variously labeled "pragmatism," "instrumentalism," "experimentalism," and "functionalism."

7. Max Fisch, ed., *Classic American Philosophers* (New York: Meredith Corporation, 1951), p. 16.

8. *Ibid.*, p. 16.

9. See Edwin G. Boring, "The Influence of Evolutionary Theory Upon American Psychological Thought," *Evolutionary Thought in America,* ed. Stow Persons, pp. 268-298.

10. Fisch, *Classic American Philosophers,* p. 24.

11. George Santayana, *Scepticism* & *Animal Faith* (New York: Charles Scribner's Sons, 1929), p. 36.

12. Fisch, *Classic American Philosophers,* p. 28.

13. See (among others) H. G. Townsend, *Philosophical Ideas in the United States* (New York, 1934), p. 134; F. I. Carpenter, "C. S. Peirce: Pragmatic Transcendentalist," *The New England Quarterly,* xiv, March, 1941, 34–48; Frederic Carpenter, *Emerson Handbook,* New York: Hendricks House, Inc., 1953), pp. 166–176.

14. Frederic Ives Carpenter, *Emerson Handbook* (New York: Hendricks House, Inc., 1953), p. 171.

15. *Ibid.*, p. 166, and also E. C. Lindeman, "Emerson's Pragmatic Mood," *The American Scholar,* xvi, 1946, pp. 57–64.

16. Cf. Max H. Fisch, "Justice Holmes, the Prediction Theory of Law, and Pragmatism," *Journal of Philosophy* 39: 85–97, Feb. 12, 1942.

17. Howard Boatwright, ed., "Introductory Note" p. xix, in Charles Ives' *Essays Before a Sonata* (New York: W. W. Norton & Co., 1964), also see p. 16, footnote.

18. Fisch, *Classic American Philosophers*, p. 7.

19. William James, *Psychology*, ed. by Gordon Allport (New York: Harper & Row, 1961), pp. 93, 94.

20. For Ives and Helmholtz, see Howard Boatwright's "Introductory Note" to Charles Ives' "Some Quarter-Tone Impressions" in *Essays*, p. 106.

21. William James, "Does Consciousness Exist?" *Classic American Philosophers*, Max H. Fisch, ed. (New York: Meredith Corporation, 1951), p. 150.

22. John Kirkpatrick, *Memos*, M8H9 (to be published by W. W. Norton, 1971).

23. William James, *The Varieties of Religious Experience* (New York: Mentor Book of the New American Library, 1958), p. 58.

24. *Collected Papers of Charles Sanders Peirce*, edited by Charles Hartshorne and Paul Weiss (Cambridge, Mass.: Harvard University Press, 1931–1935) 6 vols., 5.461; cf. 5.565.

25. Justus Buchler, ed., *The Philosophy of Peirce: Selected Writings* (New York: Dover Publications, 1955), passim.

26. Charles Ives, *Essays*, p. 71.

27. See also Leonard B. Meyer, *Emotion and Meaning in Music* (Chicago: The University of Chicago Press, 1957), p. 257.

28. Bertrand Russell, "Math, Logic, and Analysis," *The Age of Analysis*, Morton White, ed. (New York and Toronto: The New American Library, 1955), p. 199.

29. Charles Ives, "Some Quarter Tone Impressions," in *Essays*, p. 108.

30. Lawrence W. Chisolm, *Fenollosa: The Far East and American Culture* (New Haven and London: Yale University Press, 1963), p. 105. William James' interest in Japan was probably kindled by Edward S. Morse's Lowell Institute lectures of 1880–1881.

31. Sidney Lewis Gulick, *The East and the West, A Study of Their Psychic and Cultural Characteristics* (Rutland, Vermont, and Tokyo, Japan: Charles E. Tuttle Co., 1963), p. 255.

32. Willi Apel, ed., *The Harvard Dictionary of Music* (Cambridge, Mass.: Harvard University Press, 1962), pp. 541, 542.

33. Count Hermann Keyserling, *Diary I.*, trans. by J. Holroyd Reece (London: J. Cape Ltd., 1925), p. 109.

34. Ernest Fenollosa, *The Chinese Written Character As a Medium for Poetry* (New York: Arrow Editions, 1936), p. 26.

35. Lawrence Chisolm, *Fenollosa*, p. 226.

36. William James, *Essays in Pragmatism* (New York: Hafner Publishing Co., 1948), p. 147.

37. Horatio Parker, "Addresses, Essays, Lectures" 1894–1919 No. 13. Yale University, Library of the School of Music (Ma 33–P–A4) Private Printing, no date.

CONCLUSION

1. Charles Ives, *Essays*, p. 71.

Rosalie Sandra Perry is Executive Director of the Office of Arkansas State Art and Humanities, responsible for developing and coordinating many programs in all the arts throughout her state. An accomplished pianist, she earned a Bachelor of Music degree with honors at the University of Arkansas, but at the University of Texas took her M.A. and Ph.D. in American Civilization. *Charles Ives and the American Mind,* her first book, reflects her conviction that art cannot be isolated but must exist in the total human context.